BIBLICAL ETHICS IN THE 21ST CENTURY

Developments, Emerging Consensus, and Future Directions

LÚCÁS CHAN, SJ

FOREWORD BY James F. Keenan, SJ

PAULIST PRESS
New York / Mahwah, NJ

Cover design by Christina Cancel
Book design by Lynn Else

Library of Congress Cataloging-in-Publication Data

Chan, Yiu Sing Lúcás, 1968-
Biblical ethics in the 21st century : developments, emerging consensus, and future directions / Lúcás Chan.
pages cm
Includes bibliographical references and index.
ISBN 978-0-8091-4837-0 (alk. paper) — ISBN 978-1-58768-249-0
1. Ethics in the Bible. 2. Christian ethics—Biblical teaching. I. Title.
BS680.E84C435 2013
241—dc23

2013014185

ISBN 978-0-8091-4837-0 (paperback)
ISBN 978-1-58768-249-0 (e-book)

Published by Paulist Press
997 Macarthur Boulevard
Mahwah, New Jersey 07430

www.paulistpress.com

Printed and bound in the
United States of America

CONTENTS

To my two Jesuit teachers and friends
Daniel J. Harrington, SJ, and James F. Keenan, SJ

FOREWORD

If you were to have a library of Roman Catholic moral theology books and you were to distinguish those books according to themes (bioethics, fundamental ethics, social ethics, sexual ethics, virtue ethics, etc.), truly the section with the newest and the fewest books would be in biblical ethics. It would also be the most ecumenical section, because Catholic ethicists have been so dependent on the longstanding work of their Protestant colleagues.

Strange, no? Our history shows us that the moral theology of Roman Catholics previously did not depend much on the bible.

Of course, there is much in the Bible to guide us in the moral life: the Ten Commandments, the Beatitudes, wisdom literature, the proverbs, the love commandment, the parables (Good Samaritan, last judgment, etc.), and so forth. But strange as it might seem, we moral theologians did not use those rich sources until very recently.

A Little History

From the twelfth to the fifteenth century, moral theology operated on two tracks. First, there was the instruction of the pastoral practice of absolving sins and giving penances. This track actually started much earlier, around the sixth century, with the *Penitential Manuals*, first used in Ireland and eventually appearing throughout Europe. They were called "penitential" manuals because they assigned fixed penances for sinful acts organized according to the seven deadly sins.

Many of these manuals were handbooks written by abbots (and abbesses) who assigned the same penances for the same sins under the same circumstances. In this way, these confessors were considered just judges as they assigned the same proportionate penances to their community members. These manuals were fairly brief, inasmuch as they dealt with sins committed for the most part by those few Christians who confessed: mostly monks, nuns, clerics, bishops, and occasionally devout nobility.

In 1215, Innocent III imposed on the Church universal the "Easter Duty," that is, the obligation to receive communion at least once a year during Easter. To fulfill this obligation, Christians had to be in the "state of grace." Therefore, each one had to confess their sins annually so as to fulfill their Easter duty to receive holy communion. For the first time, the whole Church was involved in a sacrament—penance—which previously was practiced only by the ordained or vowed religious.

Not only did the laity have to know how to confess their sins, the clergy had to learn how to hear them. Moreover, since the sins of monks and nuns tended to focus on their vows and religious practices and were generally less complex than those of people with families and businesses, the penitential manuals became very inadequate for this much larger and more diverse group of sinners. In the thirteenth century, the much more extensive summaries of confessional material, the *Summa Confessorum,* were published. These texts did not simply aim to assign universally fixed penances; they also guided confessors to learn how to discover the sources of sin in the individual penitent. Here, then, confessors became trained, not simply as just judges, but also as physicians of souls.

At the same time, for an elite group of religious and clerics there developed a highly intellectual track of theology, known as scholasticism. These theologians (Peter Abelard, Peter Lombard, Albert the Great, Thomas Aquinas, Bonaventure, Duns Scotus, and William of Ockham, to name a few) taught at the universities recently established (think here of Oxford, Bologna, Padua, Paris). Eventually, they gathered their teachings together in tomes known as the *Summa Theologiae.*

In sum, from the twelfth to the end of the fifteenth century, there were two very different tracks of moral theology: the practical and very specific *Summa Confessorum* and the highly academic *Summa Theologiae.*

Casuistry

In the sixteenth century, Europe was bent on enormous expansionism. Westward, explorers from Portugal, Spain, France, Holland, Italy, and England began their conquest of the Americas. At the same time, they engaged in extensive trade negotiations with the East. With such new frontiers, the moral questions of the sixteenth century were altogether new.

For instance, the Church had held that usury or moneylending was always sinful. Consider maritime insurance, that is, insurance for shipping vessels. In 1237, Pope Gregory IX ruled that paying collateral fees for shipping was a form of usury, and, therefore, sinful. In the sixteenth century, Europeans needed to insure their cargoes returning from the conquest of the Americas or from trade with the Mideast and Asia. They wondered: Did Pope Gregory's ruling apply to maritime insurance or was such insurance morally licit?

In 1530, a group of Spanish merchants living in Flanders asked the University of Paris to address maritime insurance. The famous nominalist professor John Mair responded that just as the captain of a ship licitly insures that a ship moves from point A to point B, so too does a maritime insurance agent licitly insure that the worth or value of the cargo moves from point A to point B. This method, high casuistry as it was later called, was fairly universal, engaged by academics as well as confessors.

For roughly one hundred years, moralists reinvestigated every question using this inductive, analogical reasoning: every form of moneyed activity, questions of lying, property, dueling, governance, war, international law, temporal authority, and even the killing of tyrants. Every type of case was reconsidered.

The Moral Manuals

By the seventeenth century, Europeans were exhausted with the high casuistry of the previous one hundred years. Moral theologians, instead of entertaining arguments for new cases, began assembling the cases into summary statements: these became known as the *Summa casuum conscientiae*, the summary of the cases of consciences. These *Summa* became the material for the seminaries that Trent mandated (1545–1563). They later developed into sophisticated textbooks, the *Moral Manuals*, which began appearing at the end of the eighteenth century and served the Church until Vatican II.

Then, a major shift happened in the organization of the summaries of cases of consciences. Previously in the *Penitential Manuals* and in the *Summa Confessorum*, the cases were organized according to the seven deadly sins. For the *Summa casuum conscientiae*, however, they were organized according to the Decalogue. Why?

This transition first occurred in the sixteenth century in the newly minted catechisms that appeared as books of doctrinal and moral instruction for home and parish, whether Catholic or Protestant, whether by Erasmus, Luther, Calvin, or even the Council of Trent. In all these catechisms of the past as well as those of the present, like the contemporary *Catechism of the Catholic Church*, the section on moral instruction is exclusively in terms of the Ten Commandments.

The summons to turn away from the seven deadly sins to the Decalogue came from reformers, certainly Martin Luther and Jean Calvin, but also earlier Catholic reformers like Jean Gerson. They made several claims. First, unlike the seven deadly sins, the commandments claimed divine sanction: they, not the seven deadly sins, appeared in Sacred Scripture as given by God. Second, the Decalogue was a solid pedagogical tool that resisted embellishment. The seven deadly sins afforded the medieval mind the opportunity to expand and compound each sin into a multitude of sins and fellow vices. The Ten Commandments as a scriptural text needed no such expansion. They simply needed explanation. Third, unlike the deadly sins, the Decalogue was expressed with negative prohibitions and also positive prescriptions. Finally, with the possible exception of pride, the sins were primarily offensive to human life; the commandments specified prescriptions and prohibitions regarding our responsibilities toward God and humanity.

By the time the *Catechism of the Council of Trent* appeared in

1566, the tradition of the Decalogue as the organizing framework for moral instruction in the Church was settled. It remained as such into the late twentieth century.

Twentieth Century

Unfortunately, though the Ten Commandments provided the organizational structure for the *Moral Manuals,* they hardly informed those manuals. No moralist did a serious study of what the Decalogue's prohibition on stealing or killing actually meant. No one looked to see what "adultery" or "honor" meant. Basically, the commandments were no more than organizing structures that provided ten headings.

Moreover, while the Protestant cathechisms, such as Luther's, were to encourage people in the parish and at home both to avoid sin and to become good disciples of Christ, the catechism for Catholics was basically meant to teach the priest how to hear good confessions; that is, to know what belonged to sin and what did not. In other words, the commandments were used solely to organize what belonged to sin, not what belonged to virtue. Matters of becoming a good disciple were raised neither by moralists nor by the use of the Ten Commandments in the confessional.

The Bible Finally Enters as a Formative Text of Catholic Moral Theology

In 1912, something truly interesting happened. A Vatican Congregation ruled that a German commentary on the New Testament was unacceptable. The Congregation ordered that it be banned and withdrawn from sale because, in the collection, an author had argued in favor of the two-source theory for the Synoptics—a position now held by nearly everyone. The Congregation told the author and the editor that they had to leave the field of Bible, but that they had the option of changing theological disciplines. The author became a prison chaplain; the editor, Fritz Tillmann, became a famed moralist.

In 1919, Tillmann wrote his first moral theological work: *Personality and Community in the Preaching of Jesus*. In 1934, he collaborated with two other German moral theologians and wrote a volume on the idea of the disciple of Christ. Tillman's volume was a tremendous success. Seventy years after its publication, it was recognized as the first Catholic work to talk about the disciple of Christ. In 1937, he published a more accessible text for lay people, *Der Meister Ruft*. This work had an even greater impact on theological discourse. In 1960, the book was translated into English, *The Master Calls*. It presented a handbook of lay morality, not as a list of sins, but as virtues dominated by the idea of the following of Christ and guided by Scripture.

Strangely enough, as important as this work was, no Catholic moralist attempted another work in biblical ethics until the 1990s. Certainly others, most notably Bernard Häring, based much of their ethics on a Gospel-inspired ethics. But Tillmann was the only moralist who used the Scriptures as his primary text.

Then came Vatican II. In the document on priestly formation, *Optatam Totius*, the Council defined seminary education and offered a simple two-sentence statement on moral theology. This comment admonished the seminaries to incorporate the Scriptures in their study of moral theology and to embrace more clearly the virtue of charity and the role of discipleship. Since its promulgation, the paragraph has become a kind of terse manifesto of the Council's agenda for moral theology. It reads:

> Special care must be given to the perfecting of moral theology. Its scientific exposition, nourished more on the teaching of the Bible, should shed light on the loftiness of the calling of the faithful in Christ and the obligation that is theirs of bearing fruit in charity for the life of the world. (*Optatam Totius* 16)

In 1984, Paulist Press published William Spohn's remarkable *What Are They Saying about Scripture and Ethics?* With great ecumenical interests, the book quickly became a reference text for providing a typology of the various models of approaching Scripture so as to understand its moral instruction. Therein, Spohn offered six models that he described as "a sign not of scholarly chaos but of the irreducible richness of the Scripture itself."

Interesting to note, Spohn referred to Protestant biblicists and moralists who wrote in biblical ethics, but when he referred to Catholic writers in biblical ethics they were all biblical theologians, like Schnackenburg and Perkins. Certainly, there was Gustavo Gutiérrez and later liberation theologians who developed their theology out of the Bible, but they were not moralists. Still Spohn made reference to four moralists, Charles Curran, Josef Fuchs, Bernard Häring, and Richard McCormick, who suggested how they thought the Bible should be used for ethics (interestingly, he did not seem to be familiar with Tillmann's *The Master Calls*).

Spohn's small book served as an enormous catalyst that, in time, generated a great deal of work about Scripture and ethics.

Sixteen years later, Spohn published a sustained argument for his own biblical foundations for ethics. In *Go and Do Likewise*, Spohn laid out an integrated vision for a biblical ethics.

Nearly thirty years after Paulist Press published Spohn's work, you hold in your hands another Paulist Press book, written by Yiu Sing Lúcás Chan. Like Spohn's book, this book provides another historical marker for a now truly developing field called biblical ethics. Like Spohn, Chan surveys the recent literature but now, with books by Catholics and Protestants, incorporates both biblicists and ethicists. Like Spohn, he helps us to see how one book after another relates to a certain category of emphasis. But while Spohn was looking at biblical ethics just as it was beginning to emerge in Catholic circles, Chan now surveys the field thirty years later. While Spohn had a few American and European contributors, Chan has a global Church writing on the topic.

Chan goes much further than Spohn by providing a way of categorizing the contributions. He assesses them. In particular, because ethicists began to write about the "ethics" in biblical ethics, he is able to comment on, not only the "biblical" claims of biblicists writing on biblical ethics, but also on their "ethical" ones. How competent are biblicists to write on biblical *ethics*? Of course, Chan then asks the same question of ethicists but with different emphasis: How competent are they to write on *biblical* ethics?

He begins to show the achievement of biblical ethics when he notes how authors begin to recognize the need for a double competency for biblical ethics: the need for biblical exegesis as well as the need for an ethical hermeneutics to apply contemporaneously the exegetical findings.

Chan does not make his claims as a simple conceptual argument. Rather after leading us through the developments of these last thirty years, he walks with us as we encounter the different attempts that biblicists and ethicists made until *they* realized they needed each others' competency.

Thirty years ago, Spohn gave us categories to prompt both biblicists and ethicists to do the work of biblical ethics. He gave us, with these categories, a memorable incentive to move ahead.

Chan follows in Spohn's path but with a newer mandate. Now thirty years after Spohn's incentive, Chan tells us it is time to take stock of what has been accomplished and to set normative standards for what makes for "biblical ethics." He not only sets these standards (that I think will be *the* foundational norms for biblical ethics), but in doing so, he also provides a much needed and very focused guide as we forge ahead. Chan is a true pathfinder. He is very thorough and so he accompanies his norms and guidelines with a variety of exemplars who are worth following. In particular, he shows us what ethicists inclined to virtue ethics are able to do with good exegesis.[1]

It's a very compelling read, with an equally compelling argument. Paulist Press once again shapes the future of biblical ethics.

James F. Keenan, SJ
Founders Professor in Theology
Boston College

PREFACE

One may wonder: Why write another book on Scripture and ethics? A simple and straightforward answer to this question is that the present work attempts to provide a bridge between the contribution of the late Catholic ethicist William Spohn and the position that I and a few others today advance in the area of Scripture and ethics, especially in doing Scripture-based ethics. This bridging project can be understood in three fundamental ways.

First, in the foreword to the second edition of his *What Are They Saying about Scripture and Ethics?*,[1] Spohn explained that the main reason for revising and even rewriting the book was the occurrence of significant developments in the field of Scripture and ethics in the ten years following the first 1984 edition. It was a good decision.

Nearly twenty years have elapsed since the revised edition was published. Since then, there have been ongoing developments in this field by both biblical scholars and Christian theological ethicists; new authors and works emerged in the English speaking world in the past two decades, including Spohn's *Go and Do Likewise*. Many of these newer works reflect and point to concrete advancements that, as I observe, throw light on the new direction in doing biblical ethics and the use of Scripture in ethics. Since we are, I believe, on the verge of an emerging consensus, now is the time to provide a more up-to-date presentation of what is occurring in the field.

A second and related reason for writing on this subject is to supplement what Spohn intentionally left out in terms of its scope of examination. In the introductory chapter of the revised edition, Spohn made it clear that his work examines the use of Scripture in ethics by theologians and not the study of ethics in

Scripture by biblical scholars. Yet, he also acknowledged that "the line between using Scripture in ethics and examining the ethics in Scripture has become blurred by the emerging discipline of hermeneutics."[2] Indeed, hermeneutics bridges the two fields and reveals that the original ethical meaning of the text studied by biblical scholars has a controlling effect on the interpretation of the text's present-day meaning. The work of biblical scholars is thus closely related to that of Christian ethicists and theologians who develop contemporary ethical insights by employing Scripture.

Moreover, as will be reviewed throughout my work, a few contemporary scholars from either of the two disciplines (of biblical studies or Christian ethics) have begun to cross the boundary so as to engage in the other's task when doing biblical ethics. In other words, biblical theologians attempt to develop their study of ethics in Scripture within sound ethical frameworks, while Christian ethicists and theologians attempt to study the original meaning of the text prior to employing the text in their ethical inquiries for today.

It is my conviction that these scholars are each going in the right direction: a true biblical ethics or a more integrated Scripture-based ethics requires us to take exegesis seriously and interpret the text by using a sound hermeneutical framework. As a result, it is insufficient to examine solely the development of how ethicists and theologians use Scripture in their ethical enquiry. One needs to explore the development within the discipline of biblical studies as well, should a more comprehensive view of the development in the area of Scripture and ethics be obtained.

Third, like Spohn, I write from the perspective of Christian ethics and perceive virtue ethics as a worthy hermeneutical tool. However, the model of "responding love" that Spohn proposed at the end of his work, though it calls forth a wide range of virtues, does not explicitly spell out the distinctiveness of virtue theory and the role of virtue theory in the area of Scripture and ethics. Thus, my work further supplements what Spohn did not do explicitly about virtue ethics, and explores how it is actually a worthy hermeneutical tool in the area of Scripture and ethics.

This threefold task of providing a bridge between Spohn's work and the position that I and a few others today advance is laid out in this book. Chapters 1 and 2 review and critique the current attempts by Scripture scholars and theological ethicists at constructing Scripture-based ethics, focusing on New Testament ethics as an illustration. In "Chapter 3: Moving toward a Consensus," I first point out that the lengthy survey reveals an emerging consensus among scholars. Then, I suggest that a hermeneutics of virtue ethics is a very worthy method for bringing our findings to ethical expression. At the end of this book, I further point out a desideratum in doing Scripture-based ethics: from bridge-building to multidisciplinary studies and dialogue with other cultures and religious traditions.

ACKNOWLEDGMENTS

I would like to express my deepest gratitude to my two Jesuit teachers and friends, Professor Daniel J. Harrington, SJ, and Professor James F. Keenan, SJ. They have been most supportive in my academic pursuits, especially in encouraging me to publish this work and cultivate the virtue of writing and publication in the midst of teaching and other ministry.

I am most grateful to both Yale Divinity School and Woodstock Theological Center of Georgetown University for granting me Fellowships that made my initial research work possible. I am equally indebted to the Jesuit School of Theology at Berkeley/Santa Clara University and the affiliated Jesuit community that appointed me as a visiting Jesuit scholar during which I was able to finalize this manuscript. Both the faculty and staff members of the school and the members of the Jesuit community have offered me their table fellowship and communal support and, for this, I am very grateful. The same gratitude is extended to Fr. Mark-David Janus, CSP, Dr. José Enrique Aguilar Chiu, and all at Paulist Press for their interest in my book project and for making it possible.

Special thanks to a few long-term Jesuit friends from the United States and abroad—Fr. James Hurley, Fr. Alfred J. Deignan, Fr. James Gould, Fr. Caoimhín Ó Ruairc, Fr. Julio Giulietti, Fr. George Griener, Fr. Momose Fumiake, Fr. John Clarkson, as well as some contemporary Jesuit friends—Titus Tin Maung, Richard Magner, Damjan Ristic, and Gerry Clarke—and the Jesuit community in Hong Kong.

May God bless all of you!

Yiu Sing Lúcás Chan

INTRODUCTION

Building Bridges

For centuries, the use of Scripture[1] in Christian ethics has differentiated Protestants from Catholics. From a historical point of view, it is noted that "virtually every profession of faith from the Reformation contained extensive statements on the authority of Scripture over human tradition."[2] Within the Catholic tradition, since the time of the patristic period, the fathers of the Church had always insisted that Scripture is not the only source of Christian ethical wisdom and knowledge. Between the Councils of Trent and of Vatican II, human reason was the primary source of moral wisdom while Scripture was often used by the authors of theological manuals in an uncritical way, primarily as "proof texts." These manualists usually began their argument "from the magisterial teaching then in place, and worked backward to illustrate how [a] particular doctrine was originally expressed in Scripture and then how [it] was subsequently developed."[3] They grouped the scriptural texts together either to confirm or decorate an argument or moral judgment.

During the seventeenth and eighteenth centuries, some authors called for a more biblical approach to moral theology, but the attempts along this line were unsuccessful. Since the middle of the twentieth century, Catholic theologians began to "catch up." Writing in 1953, Philippe Delhaye, for example, is noted for calling for a "more positive science of moral based on Scripture and Tradition."[4] Around the same time, famous Roman Catholic manualist Bernard Häring also proposed a more biblically centered approach in his groundbreaking work on moral theology, *The Law of Christ*.

Nevertheless, the impact of the Second Vatican Council on integrating Scripture and moral theology needs to be recognized. In light of this Council, many Catholic moral theologians quoted the following statement to demonstrate the Council's effort to emphasize the biblical-theological foundations of Catholic moral theology: "Special care should be given to the perfecting of moral theology. Its scientific presentation should draw more fully on the teaching of Holy Scripture..." (*Optatam totius* 16).[5]

Both Scripture scholars and theological ethicists within Catholic circles generally welcomed this statement, and, as a result, a Scripture-based Christian ethics began to develop among these theologians.

More than forty years after the Council, the Vatican's Pontifical Biblical Commission issued a document entitled *The Bible and Morality: Biblical Roots of Christian Conduct.* Rooted in the spirit of Vatican II, it aims at situating Christian morality in the larger context of biblical morality and of anthropology and showing that the Bible does provide some methodological criteria for moral progress. The Commission is concerned with a Scripture-based morality and stresses that methodological criteria are necessary in order to allow us to refer to Scripture in moral issues.

Still, the two branches, Scripture and moral theology, as Daniel Harrington rightly observes, continue to operate separately without much cooperation, and the integration of Scripture and theological ethics is far from satisfactory: many moral theologians do not read much of what biblical scholars write, while few biblical scholars have interest in conversing with moral theologians.[6] Thomas Ogletree, however, is more sympathetic and perceives the gap as a result of a growing complexity in the two fields in terms of materials treated and methodologies devised. He claims that it is difficult enough for a specialist in Christian ethics to be dynamically connected with theological foundations of ethics, "let alone to assess the respective merits of tradition criticism, redaction criticism, and literary criticism in the study of biblical texts."[7] Sadly, some ethicists even avoid integrating the Bible into their work all together, worrying that, in practice, doing biblical ethics requires all the other theological skills.

Both the lack of interest and growing complexity in the two fields point to the concrete issues of training and communication that lead to the limited influence of Scripture on moral theology. James Gustafson rightly observes, "Those who are specialists in ethics generally lack the intensive and proper training in biblical studies, and those who are specialists in biblical studies often lack sophistication in ethical thought."[8] Regarding the lack of communication, both Christian ethicists and Scripture scholars are responsible: on the one hand, many moralists were preoccupied with natural law; on the other hand, biblical scholars "had not as yet demonstrated to the moralists the possibilities for using Scripture in moral theology."[9] This issue is best expressed in the frustration of the late Richard McCormick, SJ: "I try to keep in dialogue with Scripture scholars...However, I've found some Scripture scholars frustrating...They're not telling us everything they know!"[10] Another concrete example is cited by biblical scholar Pheme Perkins who recalls that her colleague at Boston College, ethicist Lisa Sowle Cahill, upon learning of Perkins's new project, persistently asked her to "make all this New Testament exegesis available for the reflection of the Christian ethicist."[11] Perkins thus admits that exegetes occasionally need to come out of their biblical world.

Apart from the possible mutual reluctance, other contributing factors include the disagreements about the authorization of Scripture in moral norms and the problem of language in interdisciplinary exercise—they speak different languages and operate in different conceptual worlds.

Full awareness of these concrete difficulties and the gap between the two fields thus urges us to develop fruitful connections between the two disciplines. Ogletree rightly warns that biblical scholarship will lose its pertinence if it is incapable of informing contemporary Christian questions, and Christian ethics will also lose its distinctive power if it ignores its biblical foundations. Perkins and Sandra Schneiders, both from the standpoint of biblical scholarship, likewise maintain that the images of both the first century and of the twenty-first century are needed in our theological quest. They also invite theologians to engage in biblical interpretation and not simply pick up their conclusions.

These illuminating insights of the 1980s, regarding the development of a genuine integration between biblical studies and moral theology, are best summarized in the words of Harrington and James Keenan:

> What is needed especially is cooperation at the level of interpretation or hermeneutics. Biblical scholars must try to learn the language and conceptuality of moral theology, and moral theologians need to learn the language and conceptuality of biblical studies (exegesis and biblical theology). Such cooperation can help rescue biblical exegesis from falling into antiquarianism and irrelevancy, and can at the same time help to enrich and enliven moral theology precisely as a Christian theological discipline.[12]

In the 1980s, we began to see different attempts among scholars to better bridge Scripture with Christian ethics. Still, the progress within academics has been slow. For instance, in the past two decades, the Society of Christian Ethics and the Society of Biblical Literature each published fewer than twenty related articles and essays in their corresponding journals.[13] Even though both societies set up units/interest groups in the annual conference to study the relationship between Scripture and ethics, examine how biblical interpretation and hermeneutics intersect with the concerns of ethics, and engage in interdisciplinary conversations, concrete measures to integrate the two fields still need to be undertaken.

Acknowledging that some other biblical scholars and theological ethicists have also made efforts in their own individual works, this book aims at constructing and advancing a more integrated Scripture-based ethics that is built upon the fruit of these theologians: one that demands at the same time both careful exegesis and interpretation using a sound ethical framework. I further propose the use of a particular hermeneutical tool in its construction, that is, virtue ethics. The primary purpose of this book is, therefore, a methodological one. I believe that only through careful observation of the contributions and limitations of previous scholars can we identify specific methodological insights that will rightfully shape the future of a Scripture-based ethics.

Moreover, in order to be comprehensive and culturally sensitive, the authors I choose are not only the most important and influential in their fields but some are also specifically aware of the relevance of local culture as well as the significance of contemporary theologies. Such diversity is important to our investigation: the differing backgrounds among these selected scholars reflect the reality of social change within the disciplines—we note that women, non-European, and Third World international figures have become important players in the field. This change in the social context of scholars signifies the shift of theological concerns not only from personal guidance to communal practices but also, more importantly, from communal to global awareness as well.

Still, here I must note a caveat: this is a study from the vantage point of theological ethics and not—primarily—biblical studies or Scripture. I am writing as a Catholic theological ethicist who does ethics by working with scriptural texts.

The Structure of the Book

The first two chapters deal with current attempts at constructing Scripture-based ethics, focusing on New Testament ethics as an illustration. I look at biblical scholars and theological ethicists within their own expertise. In each chapter, I first offer a brief overview of their corresponding tasks in relation to Scripture and ethics. These overviews are foundational, but not exhaustive or historical. Then, I examine how these scholars employ different methodologies and approaches in their attempts to deal with Scripture and ethics. Two male Scripture scholars from North America are important to examine: Richard Hays and Frank Matera. Apart from these two New Testament ethics scholars, feminist and non-western Scripture scholars also have attempted to study ethics in Scripture from their specific context and perspective. I review two of them: Sandra Schneiders and Rasiah Sugirtharajah. In the case of theological ethics, I examine the works of some major Christian theologians and ethicists who are representatives of their own contexts and perspectives, namely, Bernard Häring, Gustavo Gutiérrez, Rosemary Radford Ruether, and William Spohn.

For various reasons, these surveys are important building blocks upon which this work is constructed. First, this work is not grounded in pure innovation but in concrete developments within the disciplines concerned. Second, it is through careful observation of the contributions and limitations of these scholars that we can identify specific methodological insights that will shape the future of a Scripture-based ethics. Third, these specific insights are found sometimes in more than one author and constitute the actual developments toward a more integrated scriptural ethics. Fourth, in proximate terms, these surveys set the stage for the discussion that follows. I believe that it is only through engagement with these insights and developments that a more integrated scriptural ethics can be properly constructed.

While these Scripture scholars and theological ethicists are innovative in their own regards, they do not pay enough attention to the importance of the scriptural text and the importance of the hermeneutics of ethics at the same time. Thus, in the third chapter, I explore the works of biblical scholar Richard Burridge and ethicist Allen Verhey, who seem to have achieved a certain balance in their own investigations and point us in the right direction by constructing a more integrated Scripture-based ethics that attends to both the importance of the text and the hermeneutics of ethics.

At this point, I note that their works are moving toward a consensus, with two aspects. The first aspect is the view that the task of exegesis and the task of interpretation are almost inseparable in the area of Scripture and ethics. I find Verhey's construal of Scripture as a "scripted script" very helpful in portraying and understanding this aspect:[14] on the one hand, the text has been written (what Verhey calls "scripted") in a particular time by a particular writer. As such, it needs to be exegeted. On the other hand, it is a "script" to be performed by an actor, and the performance itself becomes the interpretation of it. Scripture as a "scripted script" thus highlights the reality that the two tasks are tightly related and one cannot engage in one task without the other at the same time. This view leads to a subsequent and second aspect: the growing collaboration between biblical scholars and theological ethicists in doing Scripture-based ethics, especially in terms of writing and teaching, as are the actual cases of Spohn team teaching with biblical scholar John Donahue, and, more recently, Keenan teaching with Harrington.

In chapter 4, I present the second half of my argument: the need to employ a particular hermeneutical tool in doing biblical ethics. Here, I propose that the hermeneutics of virtue ethics is a very apt method. Why? First, in the past few decades, virtue ethics has returned and become a prominent alternative to principle-based ethics. It deals with the character of individuals and their communities, as well as the practices that develop those characteristics and, in turn, express them.[15] Second, in terms of the narratives and the overall ends of Scripture themselves, we will see that virtue ethics is the most congruent and the most able to bear the weight of interpretation. Third, as Spohn explained, it is a matter of necessity to select one form of ethics, for it is not possible to explore Christian moral life without it being built upon some form of moral philosophy.[16]

I first review the hermeneutics of virtue ethics, with special attention to its revival and contemporary understanding. Here, I introduce four important dimensions of virtue ethics, namely, (1) dispositions and character formation; (2) practices and habits; (3) exemplar; and (4) community and communal identity. I also briefly discuss the issues of cultural and theological adaptation, such as contextualization and the relation between virtue and grace. Then, I look at how Scripture can be read through the lens of virtue. In so doing, I examine how two virtue ethicists read Scripture through their hermeneutics of virtue ethics. The first virtue ethicist is Joseph Kotva, who has made a Christian case for virtue ethics. Kotva establishes a link between the New Testament and virtue theory. For the second ethicist, I return to Spohn, who offered his attempts to integrate Scripture and ethics through a hermeneutic of virtue ethics. Finally, I present my own approach of relating Scripture with virtue ethics.

At the end of this book, I raise the question of what happens from here. I admit that what I have been advocating so far may be a very challenging task in the sense that it demands both biblical scholars and Christian ethicists to acquire the skill and knowledge of each other's expertise when engaging a genuine Scripture-based theological ethics. It may take some years before a new generation of Scripture-based ethics scholars is trained in this fashion. What can be done during this interim period? I take a quick look at two current, concrete cases found in the university setting as a starting point for further reflection. I close, then, with clear indications of what the future looks like in this field—one that goes beyond bridge building to integration and dialogues.

CHAPTER ONE

THE ATTEMPTS BY SCRIPTURE SCHOLARS

The Study of Ethics in Scripture: New Testament Ethics[1]

For the task of studying ethics in the Bible, biblical exegesis (i.e., the critical study of the original meaning of the text) is foundational. This exegetical task is commonly subdivided into Old Testament ethics and New Testament ethics. In the case of the New Testament, it has been customary to organize the ethical contents thematically or chronologically.[2] Still, a wide spectrum of methods and perspectives is pursued, ranging from a strictly historical approach to phenomenological analyses that surpass the distinctive religious language and context of the first century, to sociopolitical approaches that reflect on the community's embodiment of the Bible.[3]

However, research requires, not only looking at the particular biblical text, but also at its context, seeing how it is incorporated into the whole of Scripture. The New Testament canon is a collection of diverse writings over a long period of time. Consequently, the ethical contents of these writings often are equally diverse. For this reason, a few biblical scholars reject the discussion of the unity of New Testament ethics, though many others do not.[4]

The way in which the content of New Testament ethics is expressed is similarly diverse. Although they generally appear in preaching and teaching that aims at responding to specific questions or criticizing certain behaviors, these ethical statements take various forms, including prohibitions, words of wisdom, and metaphorical expressions. Many of them draw heavily on other ethical traditions, such as that of the Old Testament, wisdom literature, and Hellenistic ethical codes. Thus, one specific task of New Testament ethics is to point out how these traditional contents are given a new ground in the light of the Gospel and how, in essential parts, their intrinsic meanings are apprehended in a new way.[5] Moreover, the concrete moral teachings of the scriptural texts, like the notions of justice and peace, are also treated differently in different texts. Thus, one cannot overlook the historical and literary contexts, and the theological significance of the text.[6]

Finally, there are a number of concrete questions that one may ask in studying New Testament ethics:[7] What were the determining factors in the authors' consideration of ethical questions? What solutions were given to the Christian communities of their time? Unfortunately, since the pursuit of New Testament ethics is associated more with moral theology than with New Testament studies, its ethics sometimes ignores or even contradicts the insights and methods of New Testament study.[8]

Since the 1970s, we have seen a growing body of literature on New Testament ethics.[9] Some of it focuses on the ethics of a particular figure or theme. For example, in his writing on Luke and Acts, Luke Timothy Johnson focuses on a particular New Testament writer, writes about a particular theme (e.g., economic issues), and appropriates a particular perspective (e.g., feminist).[10] Others attempt to write on the subject in a more comprehensive manner.[11] Leslie Houlden, in his *Ethics and the New Testament*, examines each of the four Gospel writers as well as Paul and James. Jack Sanders's *Ethics in the New Testament* further expands the examination to both the later epistles outside of the Pauline tradition and the Apocalypse.

However, the works of both Houlden and Sanders are rather brief in content and scope when compared to those written in the 1980s and later. Therefore, one of the criteria for selecting biblical scholars for my review here is that the works be fairly substantive. Another criterion is that these works have contributed notably to the discipline. Finally, I look to diversity—in terms of geographical location, faith tradition, gender, and the economic status of the country from which they come—in order to provide a certain span to review the work of New Testament ethics in the past two decades. Such diversity reflects the reality of social change within the discipline: women, non-Europeans, and Third World figures enter the world stage at this time. This social change signifies the shift of theological concerns not just from personal guidance to communal practices but, more importantly, from communal to global awareness as well. The New Testament scholars I have chosen thus include Richard Hays, Frank Matera, Sandra Schneiders, and Rasiah Sugirtharajah.

Richard B. Hays[12]

Richard Hays is a Methodist and professor of New Testament. Since the early 1980s, Hays has been writing on New Testament ethics, focusing on particular Pauline writings. However, throughout the whole decade of the 1990s, Hays shifted his interest to the methodological discussion of New Testament ethics itself. Two related essays of this period are particularly noteworthy for they reveal his personal conviction regarding New Testament ethics, namely, that New Testament ethics is a normative theological discipline.

In his first essay, "Scripture-shaped Community: The Problem of Method in New Testament Ethics," Hays proposes a multitask framework in doing New Testament ethics. The need for a multifold task is grounded in the fact that "critical exegesis exacerbates the hermeneutical problem rather than solving it...[and heightens both] our awareness of the theological diversity within Scripture and our historical distance from the original communities."[13]

The first element of the threefold task is a descriptive one—basically, exegesis. Hays emphasizes the need of a "thick" description because the moral teachings of the New Testament are found not only in explicit teachings but also in the narratives, symbols, social construct, and practices that shape the ethos of the community. The second (synthetic) task aims at seeking possible coherence and unity of ethical perspective within the diverse writings. Hays warns that it is a necessary task if one has theological concerns in view in the pursuit of New Testament ethics. During this process, a cluster of images will slowly emerge. These images are "capable of providing an interpretive framework that links and illumines the individual writings" and are needed to handle tensions among the diverse canons and to ground unity for the New Testament's moral vision.[14] The third task, hermeneutics, bridging the gap between the text and ourselves, requires us to place ourselves "imaginatively" within the text's own world.

In a second essay, five years after the publication of the first, Hays added a fourth task—the "pragmatic" task—and understood the fourfold task of New Testament ethics as a *theological* one. This addition was based on two beliefs: (1) Christian ethics is "fundamentally a *hermeneutical* enterprise...[that] must begin in the interpretation of and end in the application of Scripture for the life of the faith community."[15] (2) The end of New Testament ethics is the formation of communities that live according to the Word. This pragmatic task thus aims at shaping the Christian community into living embodiments of the meaning of the texts. It also serves as a test for the capacity of the other three tasks in producing individuals and communities whose character corresponds to Jesus Christ.

Hays brings this fourfold task into his significant book *The Moral Vision of the New Testament*. As the title suggests, Hays focuses on the "ethical vision" of the New Testament and illustrates how it ought to shape the values and practices of the Christian community today. Here, the book is divided into four interrelated parts corresponding to the fourfold task.

The descriptive part surveys the major New Testament writings according to their assumed historical order.[16] The distinctive moral visions embodied in these writings are subsequently sketched. Among the Pauline writings, three theological motifs—eschatology, the cross, and the new community in Christ—that provide the cosmic, apocalyptic framework for Paul's moral vision of *koinonia* of Christ's sufferings, are highlighted. In the textual interpretation of the Gospels, Hays focuses on Christology, ecclesiology, and eschatological expectation. The Book of Revelation, however, contains a moral vision shaped by the apocalyptic eschatology that offers hope, consolation, and warrants for obedience. In each treatment, Hays takes time to illustrate "how these particular visions had concrete implications for the behavior and life of the early Church."[17] However, while Hays acknowledges the need to attend to the developmental history of moral teaching traditions, he emphasizes the shape of the whole work; thus, the approach employed is predominantly literary.

The second part of the book focuses on the discussion of the plausibility of a coherent normative New Testament ethics. While it is doubtful that a single unifying notion is adequate, Hays is convinced that synthesis is still possible and, thus, he articulates wherein the unity of moral visions lies. An inductive approach is used here. Interestingly, those three governing images identified in Pauline writings, namely, community, cross, and new creation, are restated as focal lenses in the discernment of what is fundamental in the ethical vision of New Testament as a whole.

In the third part, Hays offers hermeneutical proposals based on the examination of how selected theological ethicists have used Scripture. He discusses four modes of moral discourse—that is, rules, principles, paradigms, and symbolic worlds—in which contemporary ethicists appeal to Scripture as a basis for moral reflection. He evaluates the ways these selected ethicists employ Scripture and how it is related to other sources.

Hays carries out the pragmatic task in the last part of this book. It is basically an application of his methodological framework onto some specific ethical issues (e.g., abortion), and the provision of an action plan. The issues chosen are based on the presumption that they require different ways of drawing upon the New Testament. A concrete illustration picked up here is the discussion of using violence in defense of justice. Hays examines Matthew 5:38–48 and claims that the normative teaching of the text is nonviolent love of enemies. By evaluating the text through the lenses of community, cross, and new creation, he learns that the Christian community is called to be one of reconciliation that determines to suffer for its witness and, yet, will be vindicated by the resurrection of the dead. The reflection upon the various modes of appropriation likewise testifies against the use of violence. Finally, a normative conclusion contends that the Church is called to be a community of peace.

Hays's project has been well received by both theological ethicists and biblical scholars as a significant resource for New Testament ethics. We recognize his work for its comprehensiveness and for being extraordinary: with the insertion of parts 3 and 4, the book is able to take on the whole task from the descriptive to the normative, and from theory to practice. Hays goes beyond the level of description as other conventional biblical scholars, such as Wolfgang Schrage, have done.

Unfortunately, I am, as others are, concerned with the adequacy of Hays's discussion of the overarching content—issues of Scripture and ethics themselves; there is no discussion of the relation of ethics to moral formation within the community, and the approach is solely act oriented and not character based.

First, Hays's decision to treat the historical Jesus only briefly in his exegetical descriptive task is unsatisfying. Second, the content of the descriptive treatment itself is rather imbalanced or incomprehensive: many of the later/Deutero-Pauline writings (e.g., Colossians) and non-Pauline Epistles are barely mentioned. The Epistle of James, for example, an epistle with a moral tradition different from the Pauline tradition, is overlooked.

Third, with others, I think that the attempt to seek synthesis has the danger of neglecting voices that either do not fit his agenda or are already subsumed within the agenda. What is problematic is that it disrupts the narrative structure of the New Testament and may omit certain essentials. Fourth, the main concern is with the three proposed focal lenses. Are they adequate for embracing the diverse teachings in the New Testament? For instance, as Burridge notes, love seems crucial in relation to Jesus' ethics and is used far more often than the cross or community. Moreover, the three lenses are so similar to those images proposed in the discussion of the Pauline writings, one is forced to wonder, as Matera does, whether Paul's writing is the ultimate determination of Hays's understanding of the New Testament's moral vision. It gives the impression that Hays "is already engaged in synthesis during the descriptive task."[18]

Fifth, Harrington and Keenan's critique also deserves our attention. Hays fails to take into account the social location of the one who employs these lenses as feminists and liberation theologians do. Keenan, in particular, claims that the ability to recognize the good in Scripture does not depend on "impersonal" images/lenses but, rather, on certain fundamental internal character traits needed for the individual and the community to attend to and understand Scripture.

Finally, being a Catholic ethicist, I find a considerable lack of Catholic representation among the selected ethicists. The presence of a Catholic voice might highlight how tradition, reason, and experience, not Scripture alone, might serve as sources for ethical insight.

Nevertheless, as a whole, we can still agree with Spohn that the complexity of Hays's approach in moving from text to world is a significant contribution.

Frank J. Matera[19]

Matera's *New Testament Ethics: The Legacies of Jesus and Paul* was published in the same year as Hays's work. Matera is a Catholic priest and professor of New Testament. Like Hays, Matera also published an article on New Testament ethics (that focused on Mark's Gospel) prior to the publication of his *New Testament Ethics*. Like Hays, this article anticipates the kind of New Testament ethics to be found in his later book. In it, Matera claims that narrative has an ethical dimension and, thus, argues that "a careful study of the narrative theology...can enrich Catholic moral theology."[20] For a fuller discussion of the ethics prescribed in each of the New Testament writings, however, we have to turn to his book.

New Testament Ethics is the second of his trilogy of New Testament studies.[21] Its goal is "to describe as accurately as possible the moral and ethical vision that a given writing proposes."[22] Matera is concerned that the traditional diachronic and synchronic methods used in New Testament ethics are inadequate in handling the texts. The diachronic method, by focusing upon chronological development within New Testament ethics, digs through the layers of traditions to Jesus' moral teaching, "fragments the New Testament witness[,] and tends to devalue later New Testament writings."[23] The synchronic approach, though preserving the integrity of the New Testament, "often mutes the individual voices."[24] Consequently, we need a different approach, one that aims at revealing certain ethical principles that are consistently applied in the texts.

What is decisive in shaping the moral life of the Church is the New Testament writings themselves; hence, the approach to New Testament ethics should not be a historical reconstruction or theological synthesis of the ethical teachings of Jesus and Paul. Rather, New Testament ethics should simply examine the moral teaching *ascribed* to Jesus and Paul: "the primary object of New Testament ethics should be the writings of the New Testament."[25]

Matera does not provide a comprehensive study of New Testament ethics or recover the ethics of the historical Jesus but limits his study only to the ethical "legacies" of Jesus and Paul—the ethics of Jesus and Paul as portrayed or represented by relevant writings. He primarily employs literary and rhetorical methods in order to trace the major themes common to these writings. Moreover, the work is primarily descriptive rather than hermeneutical.

Matera basically offers us a two-part presentation, namely, the legacies of Jesus and of Paul. The legacy of Jesus is drawn from the Synoptic Gospels as well as the Johannine writings. The Synoptic Gospels are focused on the proclamation of the coming of the kingdom and, so, the moral norm is one's response to the coming of the kingdom. In John, ethics becomes Christology and the subsequent moral norm is one's response to Jesus' commandment to love one another. Still, the distinctive themes identified in each gospel tradition lead us back to Jesus. Subsequently, Matera claims that we can trace certain common moral themes in the legacy of Jesus, such as the kingdom of God, repentance, faith, love, discipleship, and judgment. In brief, although each Gospel has a different emphasis and the interpretation of these themes varies, they all manifest a common origin and hence reflect certain commonalities among them.[26]

Regarding the moral teachings attributed to Paul, Matera notes that no single Pauline writing can summarize Paul's moral teaching or stand for a systematic development of ethical theory. Each Pauline and Deutero-Pauline letter is related to its own background and underscores themes, such as election, justification by faith, and the importance of building up the community by works of love. These recurring themes are also manifested in the Pastorals despite their eschatological and ecclesiological orientations.

The concluding chapter provides a synthesis of the ethical legacies of Jesus and Paul. Although Matera does not offer any theological themes or focal images as does Hays, he identifies several general conclusions (or theses) about the shape of New Testament ethics. The moral life of believers is: (1) a response to God's offer of salvation; (2) lived within a community of disciples; (3) guided by the examples of Jesus and Paul; (4) directed toward God and toward the fulfillment of God's will; (5) manifested in our worship and our love toward others; and (6) an ultimate expression of faith. He concludes that the overall ethical teaching of the New Testament is thus inseparably connected with the message of salvation, and the entire project is a first attempt toward a systematic presentation of New Testament ethics.

Before offering comments on Matera's work, we have to acknowledge that his work has drawn broad scholarly attention. In particular, the number of reviews prompted by the book is quite impressive.[27] The general comment is positive, and many praise him for the good amount of useful information and materials offered, as well as the provision of a concise, up-to-date analysis of the materials. As noted earlier, the work is often compared with Hays's *The Moral Vision of the New Testament*. For example, with regards to the quantitative aspect of Matera's work, one commentator writes, "Hays's first section covers similar ground to Matera's monograph ...but in the material they have in common, Matera, not surprising, is frequently the more comprehensive...Matera provides a valuable alternative or supplement to Hays."[28]

Unfortunately, the quality of the contents raises our concerns. Some comment that the work reads more like a New Testament "introduction" with ethical questions in the foreground than a masterpiece that significantly advances our understanding of New Testament ethics. From the perspective of an ethicist, I too find that the ethical claims of the study are rather modest and are "not exactly what one might expect from a study on ethics."[29] A more probing and critical analysis seems to be needed. For instance, apart from repentance and faith, what kind of relationships, values, and practices does the kingdom of God demand? Even though Matera makes it clear that his task is purely descriptive, we have already learnt from Hays's own work that biblical ethics needs to move beyond mere description.[30]

What is encouraging in Matera's work is his methodological orientation. He attempts to transcend the limitations of the historical-critical method in New Testament studies. His attempt toward a systematic presentation of New Testament ethics further demonstrates his effort to reconcile the two traditional (diachronic and synchronic) approaches. For some, this new approach is not without puzzles, at least on the practical level. In the first place, one may rightly ask how he selects and categorizes the ethical contents of the writings. His chapter headings disclose his own biases: for example, why "election," instead of "suffering" is highlighted in the treatment of the two letters to the Thessalonians. Second, on what grounds should certain writings like the letters to the Hebrews and Philemon and the book of Revelation be omitted?[31] Third and last, there is a fundamental issue of the connection between the legacy of Jesus and that of Paul. Matera seems to take this connection for granted.

Sandra M. Schneiders[32]

Sandra Schneiders, IHM, a Roman Catholic religious, has been teaching New Testament and Spirituality for over thirty years. She is convinced that an interpretation that "adequately takes into account the complex nature and multiple dimensions of the text and the reader" is crucial to biblical scholarship.[33] This conviction has led her to construct "an interdisciplinary theory of biblical hermeneutics that can ground a coherent methodological pluralism."[34]

Schneiders informs us that there is a growing awareness and recognition among biblical scholars that there is no pure objectivity in exegesis, and that the biblical texts contain not only historical but also theological—as well as spiritual and moral—concerns. Within Roman Catholic biblical scholarship, Schneiders also recalls that its renewal has called for inter- and multidisciplinary interpretation of biblical texts, and highlights the growing role of the Bible in informing other theological disciplines, especially spirituality and pastoral morality.

In this light, Schneiders rightly argues that Catholic biblical scholars can "no longer [be] immune from the theological and pastoral consequences of [their] work."[35] This is very important. Earlier exegesis, unlike hermeneutics, was considered an objective, non-interpretive science. Anyone with training could exegete the same text as another could and the exegesis would presumably be the same. The social location of the exegete was not important. But Schneiders contends against this position. The exegetical task is thus important but inadequate. She notes that a text "once written is no longer determined by the understanding of the original audience [but] open to whoever can read it."[36] As a result, the ultimate object of biblical scholarship is the *contemporary* meaning of the text. Biblical scholars need to go beyond seeking what the text meant alone.

To acquire a more mature and comprehensive presentation of her insights, I turn to her two books published a decade ago, *The Revelatory Text: Interpreting the New Testament as Sacred Scripture* and *Written That You May Believe: Encountering Jesus in the Fourth Gospel*. The first one is basically a study in hermeneutics. Schneiders hopes "to elaborate a theory of interpretation that can ground a reading of the text that is unreservedly critical, on the one hand, and that interacts meaningfully with the personal and communal spiritual life of the believing reader...on the other."[37] For Schneiders, a text is "an experience which has the power to transform us in the encounter between the text and the interpreter."[38] She identifies such hermeneutical theory of biblical interpretation as the "integral" or "transformative" interpretation.

This integral interpretation deserves our attention. It begins with the understanding of the text itself. In doing so, Schneiders draws upon the hermeneutical insights of Paul Ricoeur and others and constructs a threefold schema in understanding the Bible: "the world behind the text," "the world of the text," and "the world before the text." The first is concerned "with what gave rise to the text and with the relationship of these facts to the text itself."[39] "The world of the text" focuses on the Bible as witness. It sees the text as a linguistic entity. The last of the threefold schema tries to invite the reader to enter its world and, thus, leads to a transformative experience for the reader. In simple terms, this entire schema "reflect[s] ways of understanding the text in relation to the originating experience, to the dynamics within the written text, and, then, to the activity of the reader in the circumstances of today."[40]

Moreover, since the content and form of the text are historical-theological and literary-historical, respectively, a plurality of approaches and methods must be employed in the process so as to probe the different dimensions of the text. Here, Schneiders suggests that ideology criticism is particularly important to the formation of an integral interpretation: it criticizes those ideologies "in respect to the oppressive distortion of reality" and "to protect the text from a premature appropriation by the reader."[41]

As a whole, rightly, Schneiders is praised for her investigations about the nature of exegesis and the role of theological involvement in interpretation.

Written That You May Believe was published in the same year as the second edition of *The Revelatory Text*. The main section of this book is actually a collection of articles that Schneiders wrote on the Fourth Gospel. Still, they represent a single, particular, and original approach to New Testament writings. The book can be seen as an application of (and supplementary to) what Schneiders has attempted in *The Revelatory Text*.[42]

Here, Schneiders makes it clear that the hermeneutical task is by no means a substitute of the descriptive task. Rather, what is needed is an integration of historical questions and methods with contemporary concerns and methods. It echoes Hays's argument for a multitask in biblical interpretation. Subsequently, the overall treatment of the Fourth Gospel involves four necessary operations of varying importance. The first is the use of historical criticism to investigate correctly the historical world behind the Johannine text. The second is the use of literary criticism to construe the meaning of the text in all its literary specificity. The third operation makes use of redaction criticism to analyze the theological content of the text that helps us to grasp its transformative meaning. The fourth and last is to engage the transformative potential of the text.

What adds to her insightful integral interpretation is that it is written from a feminist perspective. Feminist criticism helps to "detect and expose gender bias in the text and/or the history of interpretation and to highlight the liberating potential of the text, especially when it has been blunted or veiled by patriarchal interpretation."[43] Thus, a feminist standpoint would conclude that women in John played unconventional roles, held remarkable original relationships with Jesus, and took extraordinary initiatives within the community. Simply put, they hold an apostleship as important as the male disciples do. In the interpretation of John 3:1–15, a feminist perspective further allows us to recognize the femininity of God that has long been suppressed by the male religious establishment.

However, Schneiders, unlike other feminist exegetes, objects to the elimination of those biblical texts that abound with materials that can be perceived as morally problematic for women. A text has a surplus of meaning that interacts with the historical consciousness of the people. The meaning intended by New Testament authors is not the only meaning; and the presence of certain material objectionable for feminist scholars is not a sufficient argument for removing a passage as revelatory text or for discounting its authority.

Consequently, Schneiders believes that a hermeneutics of "retrieval"—that moves beyond suspicion—is possible for feminist criticism. In the story of the Samaritan woman in John 4:1–42, for example, a hermeneutics of retrieval that employs feminist exegetical critical strategies would, therefore: (1) challenge androcentric translations; (2) focus on "woman material" found in the text; (3) make women visible and constitutive of the text; (4) reveal what is overlooked in the text; and (5) challenge possible misinterpretations. As a result, the story of the Samaritan woman is a case of inclusive discipleship.

In sum, Schneiders's works on hermeneutics are praised for going beyond biblical criticism that concerns only the text. She guides us to see how the text leads us to the revelatory transformation of the readers. Her integral use of different biblical approaches in exegesis and her demonstration with concrete examples are innovative and thorough, inclusive and dialogical. However, the appropriateness of using ideology criticism to rid the Bible of all its ideologies for the sake of preserving its sacredness is debatable. Donald Senior further comments that Schneiders has overstated biblical scholarship's emphasis on textual objectivity.

Although Schneiders is not writing on New Testament ethics *per se* and her integral/transformative interpretation is only a preliminary sketch focusing on bridging the Bible and spirituality, I find that her works shed light on the possibility and importance of formulating a kind of biblical interpretation that is helpful in bridging biblical scholarship and other theological disciplines, like theological ethics. As noted earlier, Schneiders's construction of a transformative interpretation grows out of a deep pastoral *ethical* concern. Thus, transformation is not simply a spiritual issue but also a moral one. She applies the integral interpretation in her reflection on a specific ethical question, where she interprets certain relevant New Testament visions of discipleship, like the Christian vocation to peace, Jesus' love commandment, and the ministry of reconciliation.

Last but not least, Schneiders's works have demonstrated the importance of searching to find the meaning of a text not only for the original audience but for the contemporary one as well. I agree that her feminist approach plays the role of complementing and even challenging the traditional biblical scholarship by male authors. Thus, I now turn to another biblical scholar who employs a perspective in biblical hermeneutics that, in some ways, coincides with feminist perspectives in their mutual resistance to any form of oppression.

Rasiah S. Sugirtharajah[44]

The fourth and last scholar to be reviewed is Rasiah Sugirtharajah, a Sri Lankan and professor of biblical hermeneutics. Like Schneiders, Sugirtharajah is not writing on biblical ethics *per se*; still, he has offered an alternative perspective in biblical interpretation that I believe can be illuminating for engaging biblical ethics.

Sugirtharajah's writings and projects are predominantly focused on biblical interpretation and hermeneutics from a *postcolonial*, Asian/Third world[45] perspective. He is deeply concerned with the lack of a genuine, distinctive Asian mode of reading the Bible and, hence, attempts to work out an alternative, indigenous Asian biblical hermeneutical theory. Specifically, he searches for a hermeneutical practice that makes use of Asia's cultural and social experiences, such as colonialism, to illuminate the biblical texts.

Sugirtharajah first points out that current Asian biblical interpretation is still dominated by the Western hermeneutics that has attained general universality. Taking into account Asia's cultural and religious pluralistic contexts, he further identifies the challenges faced by Asian Christian interpreters, namely, the need to learn to appreciate and identify the differences within the context of their multi-religious texts; and the need to be aware of their identity and role in relation to the marginalized, the Church, the academy, and being diasporic, bicultural interpreters.

Consequently, Sugirtharajah attends to marginal interpretative voices and advocates the use of postcolonial criticism as the proper methodology needed for Asian biblical interpretation. In general, postcolonial studies analyze the diverse strategies by which the colonizers constructed images of the colonized and understand how the colonized made use of these strategies in order to articulate their identity, empowerment, and so forth. The advent of the corresponding critical theory or hermeneutics, however, was triggered by sociopolitical and economic events in the 1980s. Not unlike liberation hermeneutics, postcolonial criticism claims to represent minority voices.

Still, its introduction and use in the field of biblical/religious studies is rather recent—in the 1990s—mainly through the works of "diasporan" intellectuals, such as Kwok Pui-lan and Fernando Segovia. They noted that "the field of biblical studies is no longer the monopoly of white, middle-class men. The addition of Western women, men and women from outside the West, as well as non-Western minorities in the West has resulted in a diversity of method and theory, an expansion of scope of inquiry, and an explosion of interpretive voices."[46]

Since then, postcolonial criticism was advocated by its proponents as an alternative to traditional historical criticism in biblical interpretation, though its advocates do not reject the insights and contributions of the latter. Sugirtharajah, being one of its foremost proponents, has advocated the use of postcolonial criticism in biblical interpretation in many of his writings, among which are *Postcolonial Criticism and Biblical Interpretation*, and *Asian Biblical Hermeneutics and Postcolonialism: Contesting the Interpretations*, which discuss the hermeneutical theory in general, and its application in biblical interpretation in the postcolonial Asia/Third World in particular. I attempt to summarize some of the key findings here.

First of all, as a discipline, postcolonial criticism is diverse in nature due to the lack of a monolithic foundation and the various sources (e.g., cultural studies) from which it draws. Yet, all agree that, in the world of literary criticism, it "expose[s] how some literature, art, and drama were implicitly linked to…colonialism."[47] The Bible is no exception; although, in time, the Bible emerged as an instrument to criticize and condemn colonial violence and other inhumane practices by the colonists.

Second, it differs from other biblical interpretative methods during the colonial period (e.g., dissident readings by colonized reformers and dissentient readings by minorities that continue to aim at evangelizing the poor) in that it places biblical studies in a non-missionary and less apologetical context.

Third, although postcolonial criticism and biblical interpretation are two separate disciplines, postcolonial biblical criticism helps situate the former's concern (i.e., colonialism) at the center of the latter. As a result, the two disciplines are able to cooperate and address certain issues together, such as identity-related topics—like slavery. Moreover, there are overlapping areas in which biblical scholars can cooperate with the postcolonial agenda, such as textual translation. As such, postcolonial biblical criticism has two fundamental interpretive tasks: "[o]ne is to interrogate the biblical narratives and the interpretations which legitimize and reinscribe colonial interests. The other is to engage in an emancipatory reading of the texts, informed by a hermeneutics yoked to postcolonial concerns."[48]

In this light, postcolonial biblical criticism would read biblical texts via different lenses in order to comprehensively highlight and scrutinize the ideologies these texts embody:[49] for instance, a hegemonic lens reveals those internal structures within biblical narratives that support colonialism, as in the throne-succession narrative in 1 Kings 1—2. Furthermore, such biblical criticism reveals that the contemporary practices of translation are often heavily biased and pay undue attention to what the translator thinks.

Fourth, in the case of New Testament studies, postcolonial biblical criticism bears in mind that both Jesus and Paul have experienced colonialism, and, hence, it reads the texts with certain characteristics. For example, in the parable of the tenants in Luke 20:9–18, postcolonial criticism attends to the reaction of the people (whose response is "God forbids") and reveals their concerns that they will be at the mercy of the new owner once the land is taken away from them. Moreover, a postcolonial reading does not romanticize or idealize the poor but discloses the system of domination (e.g., the "generous" widow in Mark 12:41–44 is viewed as a woman manipulated by the political system). Postcolonial biblical criticism further pushes for a broader hermeneutical agenda that interprets the texts within the intersecting histories that constitute them (e.g., Christian-Hindu interaction) and within an inter- and multi-textual perspective.

In order to illustrate these points more coherently, I turn to Sugirtharajah's own commentary on the three Letters of John. In the first place, postcolonial biblical criticism would identify the colonial discourses in the epistles: (1) the author's intolerance of theological dissidence and the subsequent use of harsh language and tone to denounce opponents (1 John 2:18); (2) his appeal to one's own credibility to maintain his own hegemony (1 John 1:1–3); (3) the stress on the authenticity of his message for the fear of unscripted improvisations (2 John 9–11); (4) the legitimization of his power by conferring on those who are on his side the identity of God's elected people (1 John 4:6); (5) his projection of an "imperial" Christ that tends to suppress other cultures and even religions (1 John 4:14); (6) the provision of hospitality and generosity only to those who agree with his position as a way to eliminate opponents (2 John 10); and (7) the use of threat and flattery to divide the community (1 John 4:4).

Postcolonial biblical criticism further recognizes two colonial frameworks within these epistles: the use of ethical dualism (e.g., light/darkness in 1 John 2:7–11) to discredit the opponents and, hence, justify control and conversion, and the introduction of father-child relationship that promotes domination, discipline, inequality, and conformity (1 John 2:18, 28). It is at this point that we see how critical postcolonial biblical criticism can be.

However, a postcolonial reading not only identifies those colonial discourses or frameworks but also offers new perceptions. It sees connections and complementary theological influences with religions/cultures other than the Jewish/Greek milieu, such as the possible influence of Buddhism on the doctrine of indwelling (1 John 4:4, 15–16). Postcolonial criticism also calls for religious activism that has communitarian and ethical implications (1 John 2:29). Moreover, it discloses the possible presence of postcolonial traits within the texts, such as textual coalitions and the author's equal emphasis on exhortation and ethical engagement.

As a whole, like others, I respect Sugirtharajah for making connections between religious/cultural imperialism and economic colonization. To the predominant hegemonic biblical scholarship, he offers a salutary alternative framework—a framework that attends to the impact of colonialism upon our interpretation. In particular, just as liberation theology did to Latin Americans, Sugirtharajah's framework challenges Asian readers and scholars to reconsider their reading of the Bible. Moreover, I fully agree that his works have offered a concrete, positive response to those who insist that postcolonial biblical criticism "should not be satisfied with simply exposing imperial tendencies in canonical texts and deconstructing them, but should go further to construct interpretations which have decolonizing effects in the contemporary world."[50]

Moreover, being an East Asian from a colonial background, I appreciate Sugirtharajah's honesty that one cannot simply employ postcolonial biblical criticism to any context, including an Asian context, without caution or suspicion. His confession somehow leads someone like me to ask if such a postcolonial criticism can really help Asian biblical scholars to know their identity, and to question if it is only a transitional term.

Nonetheless, Sugirtharajah and his postcolonial biblical criticism, not unlike the case of feminist theology and its hermeneutics, have raised serious methodological questions that have a strong impact on the overall enterprise of biblical studies, including the area of New Testament ethics. Specifically, we recall that the purpose of postcolonial biblical criticism is not to rediscover the Bible as an alternative for a better world but "to puncture the Christian Bible's Western protection and pretensions, and to help reposition it in relation to its oriental roots and Eastern heritage."[51] In our own quest of New Testament ethics, it provides a "location for other voices, histories and experiences to be heard" so that new insights and methodology to the ethical teachings of the Bible may emerge.[52]

So far, I have surveyed how Scripture scholars have tried to construct a methodological framework for biblical ethics that is built upon their particular perspectives. Each of them has provided certain specific methodological insights in their dealing with New Testament ethics although their specific insights are found sometimes in more than one author. Their overall contributions can be summarized in two areas.

First, the scriptural text is important to our construction of a Scripture-based ethics and so we need to take the text seriously. Subsequently, we need to keep a balance between seeking unified themes among the texts and respecting their diversity so as to be truthful to the texts. Likewise, the exegetical task needs both to go beyond traditional critical methods and to employ different approaches that attend to the social, cultural, and religious background of the text, and even the philosophical theory behind the text.

The second area of contribution I observe is that Scripture-based ethics requires not just exegesis but more importantly an appropriate hermeneutics that is concerned with the meaning of the text for today. This hermeneutical task needs to acknowledge and be attentive to the interpreter's social location; hence, alternative hermeneutical methods relevant to one's perspective are needed.

Despite the recognition of their insights and contributions, we also see certain limitations in the attempts of these scholars that continue to challenge us to seek further development. I identify three related criticisms. The first is that the ethical claims identified in their writings are, broadly speaking, rather modest, general, and at times inconsistent or over subjective. I find that both Hays's focal images and Matera's theses on New Testament ethics are only general statements and sound more theological than ethical. There is also a lack of critical analysis of these claims. Similarly, exegetes show a lack of critical reflection of their own ethical self-understanding and social location, which Keenan, Schneiders, and Sugirtharajah have rightly raised. It is a crucial and necessary step if the exegete is to do biblical ethics in the twenty-first century.

A second criticism is that there is almost no reference to or consultation of the works of theological ethicists (ancient, medieval, or contemporary) when making those ethical claims. Even when Schneiders adopts the insights of other scholars, she is narrowly focusing on their contributions to philosophical or feminist discussion alone.

Flowing from this, the last and most foundational criticism is a methodological one: their ethical claims either have no direct and sustained reference to, or are not built upon, any major ethical theories (e.g., natural law theory). One wonders on what bases do they make their ethical claims? While they rightly call for the need of hermeneutics to bridge the text and today's readers, they fail to demonstrate this task on solid ground. As a result, it raises concerns about the overall accuracy of their ethical claims and the effectiveness of their overall methodological attempts.

In short, these biblical theologians still stress the importance of the scriptural text, while basically neglecting the ethical hermeneutics needed to interpret the texts on an ethically normative level.

CHAPTER TWO

THE ATTEMPTS BY THEOLOGICAL ETHICISTS

The Use of Scripture in Ethics

Contemporary Christian ethicists suggest four separate and yet related tasks in using Scripture in ethics, namely, the exegetical, hermeneutical, methodological, and theological tasks.[1] The first two are shared by New Testament scholars. This commonality affirms that exegesis is important if the Bible is to serve as an ethical resource. Moreover, the issue of interpretation is inevitable, for the Bible is historically conditioned and new questions emerge from each generation. The methodological task asks how one employs Scripture within the various levels of moral reflection. James Gustafson notes that how a Christian ethicist uses Scripture is determined by how one defines the task of Christian ethics, and, from there, he famously distinguishes the Bible as "revealed morality" from "revealed reality."[2]

The fourth and last task—the theological one—mainly concerns meta-ethical questions, such as the authority of Scripture in moral guidance. Although the state of these questions has shifted in the past forty years (e.g., from the authority of the Bible in establishing norms to the role of Scripture in forming vision/values and communities of discipleship), the discussions and claims made then are foundational to the overall quest. Scholars continue to address them today.

Regarding the Bible as a source of Christian ethics, for instance, more and more Christian scholars would adopt John Wesley's view that there are actually four sources, namely, Scripture, tradition, human reason, and experience. Few think of the Bible, however, as the only source for Christian ethics to the point of making our ethical decisions. Unfortunately, in practical terms, these sources are in tension.[3] Those who hold a middle ground thus propose a dialogical relationship among the sources, and claim that Scripture and other sources are often, in fact, quite indistinguishable from one another.[4] Others argue for some sort of prioritization and, as expected, they propose the primacy of Scripture.[5]

Scripture as a source of ethical reflection claims certain legitimate authority. Yet, there are diverse attitudes toward its authority. Some claim that biblical authority is neither absolute nor exclusive but relational (or even hierarchical) to other nonbiblical authorities.[6] Others, like Stanley Hauerwas, would argue that the Bible does not have authority apart from the community of believers, and its authority is "for and in the Church." Lisa Sowle Cahill is more nuanced. For her, it is a "faith" decision when one uses Scripture as an authority. Thus, biblical authority needs to be understood as "authoritative pattern, structure, or form [instead of]... 'substantive canonical authority'."[7] From a different angle, Kenneth Himes points out that acknowledging the Bible as authoritative does not mean it functions in an authoritarian way; rather, it means Scripture is an essential source for moral discernment.[8]

While Scripture is a resource for solving moral issues, the above discussion reveals that the Bible is also a source of moral problems.[9] Since the early nineties, the problem has been an issue of diversity.[10] First, there is the basic internal diversity; we must recognize that the Bible is a collection of books written in different historical and sociocultural circumstances over a long period of time. There exist diverse perspectives among which inconsistencies and even contradictions are found. Second, these various perspectives and teachings are further manifested via different literary forms that are historically and culturally conditioned, and, hence, they cannot be treated as free-floating principles. Third, even some of these meanings could be erroneous, whether by fact or by value, as in the case of the household codes today challenged by feminists. Fourth, Scripture speaks neither clearly nor directly to, and cannot adequately deal with, the new issues that are peculiar (and/or important) to our contemporary world.

Apart from these major problems, there are other practical issues as well, such as the tension of providing moral wisdom from a single Scripture for people of divergent historical and cultural backgrounds, the difficulty of applying a religious ethics to secular debates, the use of ancient languages, and the subsequent need of exegetical skill.[11]

Nevertheless, these obstacles have not stopped Christian ethicists from employing Scripture in moral reflection. In fact, prior to Philippe Delhaye's call for a Scripture and Tradition–based moral theology in 1953, German Catholic moral theologian Fritz Tillmann had already attempted to develop a Christian ethics based on Scripture, and his work influenced a series of subsequent German authors, such as Johannes Steinberger and Häring.[12]

Since then, more and more moral theologians and ethicists, such as Edward Leroy Long and David Kelsey, began to advocate the use of Scripture and have written important articles on the use of the Bible in Christian ethics.[13] Based on the same criteria—in terms of the selection of scholars and areas of evaluation—set out in the previous chapter, I will review the following theological ethicists in their use of Scripture in Christian ethics: Bernard Häring, Gustavo Gutiérrez, Rosemary Radford Ruether, and William Spohn.[14]

Bernard Häring[15]

Bernard Häring (1912–1998) is remembered as one of the most influential moral theologians of the twentieth century, especially for reshaping Catholic moral theology.[16] Although he was identified as a moral "manualist," he brought many new ideas to Catholic moral theology prior to and during the Second Vatican Council through his writings and active participation in those conciliar commissions. Among these new insights is the integration of scriptural references into moral discussion—Häring perceived both the Bible as the central source of moral theology and moral theologians as mediators of biblical messages and tradition. In his multi-volume *The Law of Christ* (*Das Gesetz Christi*), Häring stated clearly that his work "attempts to expound the most central truths in the light of the inspired word of the Bible."[17] He also claimed that the presentation of the content and specific characteristics of New Testament law is a major task of moral theology. As mediator of the biblical message, moral theologians, therefore, should be nourished by the Word of God and learn from the work of biblical scholars. He said, "Moral theology, as I understand it...its basic task and purpose is to gain the right vision...by listening to the word of God."[18] Many believe that this work set off changes that the Second Vatican Council sought to bring about.

Another important role Häring played in Vatican II was his involvement in the drafting of the earlier quoted *Optatam totius*. He was even referred to as "the quasi-father of *Gaudium et Spes*."[19] Häring's insights continued to influence Catholic moral theology well after the Second Vatican Council.

Although Häring advocated the integration of Scripture into moral theology, his more mature view of biblical authority in moral reflection grew only slowly over his career. In his earlier writings, Häring made a great distinction between the authority of the Old Testament and that of the New Testament, so much so that he perceived the authority of the Old Testament as completely transcended by the New Testament law. Only much later did he assign a greater authority to the Old Testament.

Nevertheless, Häring claimed that normative statements (e.g., the Sermon on the Mount in Matt 5–7) alone are authoritative and binding although those concrete, time-bound passages (e.g., Paul's statements about women's veils in 1 Cor 11:2–16) can still be helpful as "models" for dealing with particular traditions in our present time.

Moreover, what makes Christian morality distinctively Christian is the normative nature of the Bible. He said, "[Moral theology] finds its distinctively Christian quality in the light of the dynamic dimensions and perspectives which we find in the

Bible. Their normative value is quite different from any kind of norms fitting external controls. They are, however, binding—and at the same time liberating—guidelines, norms in a very broad but real sense. They depend thoroughly on faith and thus are distinctively Christian."[20]

Later on, Häring was convinced that Scripture not only informs but also forms the community into one of a particular character, and it is in this sense that Scripture is authoritative. The Bible contains reflections and internal thought patterns (e.g., virtues) that can shed light upon our Christian life. Consequently, Scripture's significance for moral theology and Christian ethics is the provision of a holistic vision of Christian life. He wrote, "We can gain the necessary vision of wholeness only by listening to the word of God and, in light of his word, searching the signs of the times."[21] Such a perception allows freedom in the biblical witness and flexibility in how Christians pursue those commands in the Bible. It also has a strong impact on his subsequent use of Scripture.

I take Jeffrey Siker's view that Häring's use of Scripture has several characteristics. In the first place, unity rather than diversity of the Bible is emphasized, particularly the call to creative liberty and fidelity and our response.[22] Second, as noted earlier, the authority of the New Testament (and the law of Christ in particular) is highlighted. This Christocentric approach explains his relatively little use of the Old Testament. Still, he drew materials from the Old Testament, such as Genesis (especially the creation story), wisdom literature, and a few prophetic writings (e.g., Isaiah). Third, as for the New Testament, in general, John is used most often. Specifically, the farewell discourse and the high-priestly prayer in John 13–17 (as well as the Sermon on the Mount in Matt 5–7) are core to his works while certain Pauline writings (e.g., Rom 5–8) and 1 John 1–5 are also frequently cited. However, Häring rarely referred to those Synoptic narratives of Jesus although he understood that the life/death and ministry of Jesus are crucial to the understanding of Jesus' moral teachings.

Regarding *how* these biblical texts are actually treated, four basic ways are further identified. First, Häring used the Bible for proof texting. For instance, he used Genesis 2:24 to back up his argument for the indissolubility of marriage. This fashion of using Scripture could be because of his identification with the manualist tradition that tends to employ Scripture to support conclusions that had been arrived at in the natural law tradition. As Siker observes, Häring himself actually acknowledged such usage in *The Law of Christ* and hoped to use Scripture in a more responsible way in his later writings.

Häring's insistence to go beyond this approach is partially grounded in his awareness that Scripture contains many key themes and images that can be used for theological elaboration and development. In this way, Häring—like Gérard Gilleman—adheres to the model that seeks to find, in their moral manuals, key biblical themes that would help their moral approach stay focused. One particular theme he favored is "freedom and creative fidelity in Christ," which inspired the title of his next major work, *Free and Faithful in Christ: Moral Theology for Clergy and Laity*.

This leads to the second use of Scripture, similar to those Word studies employed among biblical scholars of the 1950s: one discusses certain theological themes or concepts by simply searching for relevant biblical texts. For example, in both *The Law of Christ* and *Free and Faithful in Christ*, Häring repeatedly studied the biblical concept of conscience under the titles of "Conscience in Holy Scripture" and "The Biblical Vision of Conscience," respectively.

A third and related use is to treat the Bible as a source of textual examples so as to illustrate certain principles or as an analogy to interpret contemporary issues. For instance, Häring claimed that African polygamists could be temporarily tolerated based on the analogy of levirate marriage in Genesis 38. He explained, "[It] should not be excluded that the text might be a challenge to the Church when she prohibits the fulfillment of the levirate duty to African tribes who are, as much as were the sons of Abraham, convinced that this is their duty."[23]

Lastly, Häring seemed to use Scripture to (what Siker calls) "season" his discussion: although he cited biblical texts to add insight to an argument, he did not develop the text or make any reference to the context. A concrete example is the discussion of the role of complementarity between men and women, where he simply cites a group of texts in which women are involved despite the diverse contexts of these scriptural passages (e.g., Mark 3:35, 7:24–30; Luke 7:36–50, 8:1–3).[24]

Regarding the task of hermeneutics, it was not until the publication of *Free and Faithful in Christ* that Häring discussed (though briefly) the issue. He said, "Hermeneutics requires knowledge both of that time and our time, sharp awareness of the biblical horizon for understanding, including the time-bound worldview of the inspired writers, and of our own culturally conditioned way of approaching the problems."[25]

In other words, careful exegesis is crucial to and a priori to applying what the Bible says to our contemporary moral issues. Häring added that the Holy Spirit plays an important role in hermeneutics: "The Spirit introduces us not only to an understanding of the Bible but…to an understanding of 'things that are coming.'"[26]

As a whole, Häring's works are applauded for highlighting the importance of the Bible in Christian moral life and integrating Scripture into moral reflection. He has also rightly argued for an active role of Scripture in Catholic moral theology. His use of biblical texts is impressive in terms of quantity. In addition, he has demonstrated some of the various uses of Scripture in moral theology. In short, Häring was an exemplar for the post-Vatican II theological ethicists in constructing a Scripture-based ethics.

Among the critical evaluations by commentators, I find a couple of them noteworthy for our methodological reflection. First, against his own call for sensitivity, Häring did not pay enough attention to those historical, social, or literary contexts of the texts he employed. Both his overly selective use of biblical texts and the lack of discussion of the various contexts in which the texts developed are recognized as "his way of ignoring those aspects of Scripture that are problematic [e.g., historical problems]."[27]

Following from this, Häring rarely engaged in actual exegesis of the selected texts and did not incorporate the findings of biblical scholars into his discussion. Third, he was over-concerned about constructing a unified biblical vision of wholeness so much so that he often ignored the diversity of approaches (e.g., the prophetic approach) within Scripture. This double avoidance of the problematic texts and of the diverse approaches, as well as the lack of exegesis, might reveal his inability or disinterest to confront those texts that may condone (or even exhort) behaviors that are against the kind of free and responsive loving act he identified in Christ.

Finally, as noted earlier, Häring did not develop or comment on those cited texts. Such methodology is thus closer to homiletical and decorative use of Scripture than anything else. Still, he brought the Bible into moral theology and realized he needed to do more than proof texting.

Gustavo Gutiérrez[28]

Peruvian Gustavo Gutiérrez has played an important role in the evolution of liberation theology through his writings and activities, especially through his active participation at the historic Medellín meeting in Columbia in 1968. Although Gutiérrez is not an ethicist or a moral theologian *per se,* his theological enquiry always has ethical implications. His seminal work, *A Theology of Liberation,* for example, is noted for bearing his ethical concerns. One ethicist writes, "On the moral level, [Gutiérrez] seeks greater clarity on how God's presence motivates the human heart and converts unjust social structures."[29]

Still, Gutiérrez's theology is not only related to ethics but to Scripture as well. He says, "In my writings I try to do theology with a strong biblical basis...I have always thought it very important to be attentive to the role of challenger that [S]cripture plays when read in the church."[30] Indeed, although his earlier works made use of social sciences, his later works (e.g., his commentary on the Book of Job) are guided by biblical exegesis. Scripture scholar John Meier thus commented that liberation theology is a concrete example in the contemporary world that "best exemplifies the promises and pitfalls of using the Scriptures as a source for theological reflection."[31]

Nevertheless, Gutiérrez's emphasis on Scripture is closely tied to his understanding of the task of theology: theology is "the critical reflection on the Christian praxis in light of the word of God."[32] The Bible is basically this Word of God that provides a foundational direction for all Christian action and reflection and has social and political significance. It is an indispensible source, revealing not just God but also humanity. Specifically, it reflects God's preference for the weak and the marginalized in human history; thus, Scripture gives us the deepest meaning and complete fulfillment regarding the notion of liberation.[33]

For Gutiérrez, Scripture as a source needs to be linked to other nonbiblical sources in a complementary way, especially with Christian praxis and social analysis. However, as far as theological and moral matters are concerned, the Bible speaks with the highest authority. This conviction is built upon the presupposition that justice is rooted in God's revelation that is authoritatively articulated in the Bible. Therefore, biblical authority is understood as challenging the oppressive authority (including ecclesial authority) and pointing toward a liberating authority.

Regarding his approach toward Scripture, Siker rightly comments that Gutiérrez is very critical of the kind of exegesis that is First World and Western oriented and that unconsciously reinforces the status quo. Gutiérrez writes, "We cannot forget that in reality, the Bible was read and communicated from the dominating sectors and classes. This is what happens to a great deal of the exegesis considered to be scientific."[34]

Thus, Gutiérrez not only pays attention to the biblical experts but also to what the community of faith says in light of its situation. He takes into account the authority of the interpreters (not just exegetes) seriously and advocates the use of other sources (e.g., critical reason) as key resources for relating Scripture to certain matters (e.g., politics). Yet, he cautions against the direct application of biblical norms to these issues because of their complexities and the composite nature of the Bible.

Gutiérrez uses both the Old Testament and the New Testament rather equally: within the Old Testament canon, Exodus, Deuteronomy, the Psalms, Isaiah, Job, and passages that speak about the oppressed/poor (e.g., Jer 20:13) are frequently cited. In the New Testament, Matthew and Luke are mostly used. And the single most frequently cited text is the parable of the last judgment in Matthew 25:31–46. Together with other similar passages (e.g., the reversal motifs in Luke 4:16–30) they highlight God's preferential option for the poor and emphasize the need for concrete and material actions.

In general, four aspects of his use of Scripture should be noted. First, Scripture is used in conjunction with human experiences that shape our identity and self-understanding as believers. For instance, he perceives the Book of Job as all about Job's personal experience through which Job's understanding of God and faith in God is reformulated and transformed. And Job's experience can be connected with our experience among the poor.

Second, biblical texts are often used to illustrate two guiding themes presented in the Bible, namely, creation/salvation and eschatology. Gutiérrez turns to the parable of the last judgment in Matthew 25 and the exodus experience to emphasize that the theme of eschatology points to the fulfillment of the salvation already begun in creation and is thus crucial for understanding the Christian faith.

Third, Scripture is used as a primary source to discern the genuine meaning(s) of poverty. We note that, for Gutiérrez, the poor find their own story in the Bible. Yet, the Bible condemns a scandalous material poverty but praises spiritual poverty that calls for complete availability to the Lord, and joins Christ in protesting against poverty and expressing solidarity with the poor (e.g., Matt 5:3–12). Here, Gutiérrez again uses the texts in light of Matthew 25.[35]

Finally, the Bible is used to initiate a dialogue between the biblical writers' foundational communities and those of the readers, so that new experiences/questions can be formed, which in turn lead to further dialogues.

From the specific perspective of Christian ethics, Gutiérrrez's use of the Bible can be understood as follows: Scripture (e.g., the parable of the last judgment) is used to call for transformation of the moral agent into one who opts for the poor in concrete acts as an expression of the love for God. Biblical texts are also employed to provide criteria for ethical judgment, to "criticize a theological-ethical system, and...to give a theological grounding to human goods."[36] The complaints of Job, for instance, become analogously the protesting word of Latin Americans against unjust systems. Finally, Scripture provides a theological basis for certain moral virtues (e.g., the transformed Job is an exemplar of the virtues of love and justice).

Gutiérrez basically employs a kind of "hermeneutical circle" that constantly reinterprets the Bible based on social analysis of one's concrete life situation and historical praxis so as to construct a new praxis. The point of departure is the historical person of Jesus who was born as a poor person among the oppressed people. In this way, biblical hermeneutics is primarily Christological.

However, Gutiérrez's hermeneutics could also be communitarian, historical, and "militant" (using Siker's terminology): as communitarian, Gutiérrez emphasizes the need to interpret the Bible in the context of faith communities; as historical, he finds within biblical interpretation an interaction between the historical experiences of both the author and the reader; as militant, he understands interpretation as starting with the struggles of the poor and calling for active commitment to the concrete service to the poor. In short, a radical approach toward the interpretation of the Bible is advocated here.

As a whole, Gutiérrez is praised for his ability and skill as biblical scholar and interpreter for today's world. Some find his use of Scripture appropriate and effective, especially in developing the principle of preferential option for the poor. He is also noted for taking the scriptural text seriously and, at times, engaging in actual exegesis.

Some ethicists further praise him for integrating the Old Testament with the New Testament (e.g., relating the Psalms and Exodus to the death and resurrection of Jesus) smoothly, as well as seeking coherence in using Scripture, as in the case of reconciling "the just avenger" image of God and "the merciful defender" image of God in the Book of Job. Moreover, he is in dialogue with contemporary biblical scholarship in his exegetical task.

However, his use of Scripture also receives severe criticism. The Congregation for the Doctrine of the Faith, in particular, criticized him for selective, incomplete, rereading of Scripture (e.g., the exodus event and the magnificat of Mary).[37] In simple terms, Gutiérrez is criticized for insisting on an over-political reading of the Bible (even though some readings are indeed more political than others). Others are also concerned that Gutiérrez might have wrongfully used the exodus story to advocate a political paradigm that does not lead to conquest of others.

Both criticisms lead to questions about his exegetical skill, his use of problematic or "bad" texts and narratives in the Bible (e.g., those that promote violence). Like Häring, he seems to avoid any confrontation with these texts.

Finally, Gutiérrez is applauded for dialectically relating Scripture with Christian praxis and, hence, makes the Bible "a book of life" for all. Yet, a fundamental problem in Gutiérrez's approaches to Scripture is spotted: he seems to hold two contradictory approaches. On the one hand, Gutiérrez's emphasis on the interpreter's experience or perspective implies relative subjectivity in the reading of the Bible; on the other hand, he seems to seek and use objective language of interpretation (e.g., the view that material poverty is evil) to evaluate other interpretations.

Despite the criticisms by the hierarchy and other scholars, Gutiérrez's overall emphasis on the interpreter's experience and the experience of the faith community could offer opportunities for seeking more truthful readings of the Bible. And his actual prophetic engagement with the texts and biblical scholarship reflects a development way beyond the manualists' approach.

Rosemary Radford Ruether[38]

Rosemary Radford Ruether has been recognized as one of the founders of the modern feminist movement in religion.[39] She aims at searching for a feminist religious revolution and advocating a critical principle that, like that of liberation theology, is anthropocentric in focus—the promotion of the full humanity of women.

Strictly speaking, Ruether is not an ethicist. Yet, her ethical standpoint can be found among her many writings, such as her analysis of socialist feminism in *Sexism and God-Talk*. Likewise, although Ruether is not a biblical scholar, she understands Christianity as (at least partially) a "biblical religion," and, thus, turns to the Bible and offers a feminist critique of it.[40] Elsewhere, she also attempts a feminist interpretation of the Bible. Therefore, it is worthwhile to revisit her use of Scripture in feminist theology and in relation to Christian ethics.

Ruether has perceived the Bible from the start as "the record of various human experiences seeking to articulate visions of faithfulness to God."[41] However, Ruether's feminist perspective leads her to recognize the incompleteness of Scripture—that is, what women know about women from the Bible is greatly restricted by what patriarchal men allow them to know. She also identifies two types of religions/traditions in Scripture that are in constant tension and dialectic relationship. The first is one of status quo within which social and ideological superstructures of patriarchy are maintained (e.g., the presumed definition of God as patriarchal male). These ideologies conceal the liberating content of the Bible. The second type is a constructive, dynamic prophetic faith through which those patriarchal ideologies can be constantly critiqued and discerned according to the contexts of the faithful. This biblical self-critique is identified as the "prophetic critique" that is rooted in the prophetic-liberating tradition.

Ruether further perceives the prophetic-liberating tradition as the central tradition of the Bible. Only that which is rooted in this tradition is normative for biblical faith.

Ruether then argues that the Bible is a source for feminist theology if and only if the prophetic principle "[implies] a rejection of every elevation of one social group against others…, [and] every use of God to justify social domination and subjugation."[42] Subsequently, the Bible is authoritative only to the extent that its texts reflect this normative critical prophetic principle. Still, one finds no final authority within Scripture for various reasons.

Among them is that it is human experience that provides the ultimate norm for biblical authority. From the feminist perspective, women's experience in particular is normative. In order to make women's experience visible, noncanonical texts are needed (since the present biblical canon is designed to silence women's voices). Therefore, Ruether seems to suggest that the Bible's prophetic principle must operate in conjunction with different principles (e.g., philosophical principles) found in other sources.

In general, the Old Testament texts that Ruether cites can be categorized into several groups, such as the creation/fall stories (Gen 1–3) and the prophetic literature (e.g., Amos 5; Hos 2). In the New Testament, those frequently used texts are similarly categorized into different groups, including texts that show women's subordination to men (e.g., Eph 5:22–24) and the sayings of Jesus that stress servanthood and anti-establishment (e.g., Matt 20:25–28, 23:1–36).

But how are these texts actually used? Ruether acknowledges that feminists face the dilemma of using Scripture to "critique tradition and suggest an alternative way of relating experience and tradition, including [S]cripture."[43] Yet, she emphasizes that feminist theology is not repudiating the tradition but simply working to liberate it from patriarchy. Thus, Ruether makes use of several biblical traditions to portray a renewable and liberating prophetic Christian faith that contains ethical responsibilities.[44]

For example, in the Old Testament, the exodus tradition is used as a liberation model for women and the transformation of the institutional Church community. The jubilee tradition (in Leviticus) is employed to remind and provide a model for the contemporary world to continue to restore righteous and just relationships that empower the powerless.

In the New Testament, the historical Jesus tradition (e.g., his treatment of women in Luke 10:38–42) is employed to highlight the need and role of prophetic critique and the promotion of a this-worldly kingdom that undoes oppression. The Pauline tradition (e.g., Phil 2:6–11; Gal 3:28) further points to the rejection of systems of domination and the ethical implication of self-emptying of the powerful in the service of the poor. The Mary Magdalene tradition (John 20:11–18) challenges the Church's conventional perception of women and its deformation of Jesus' prophetic and liberating message into a new status quo of hierarchy.[45]

Still, Ruether understands the task of hermeneutics as both a dialectical process and a circular task with human experience as its starting point and ending point. From the feminist perspective, this experience refers particularly to women's experiences as created by a male-dominated society and culture. The awareness of this unique experience, as well as the self-affirmation as autonomous persons capable of self-determination in all relations, is crucial to a feminist hermeneutical method.

According to Ruether, there is a *correlation* between the feminist critical principle and the biblical critical/prophetic principle:[46] feminist hermeneutics is basically "the feminist radicalizing of the prophetic tradition" and "the feminist interpretation of prophetic critique [of Scripture]...in the context of new communities of critical consciousness."[47] What is innovative is "feminist's appropriation of this norm *for women*."[48] It understands no human constructs of thought are absolute and infallible, and, hence, its formulations must be constantly evaluated by the appropriated theories.

This self-critique leads us to a critical evaluation of her use of Scripture.[49] It can be divided into three areas: selection of text, interpretation, and methodology. First, some find her selectivity well-grounded in history. Others, however, comment that her use is at times too selective. Moreover, her suggestion that new texts need to be selected for a working canon so that women's experience could be visible is seen by some as problematic. What are, for example, the criteria for the selection of these new texts? Or, will not the new working canons themselves sacralize the specific experiences and understandings of those who select the texts?

Second, many commend her for appropriating the prophetic tradition for women in particular (e.g., her interpretation of the biblical condemnation of idolatry). Some, however, provide contrary comments. For instance, they wonder if Ruether's interpretation of Jesus as an iconoclastic teacher/healer is shaped by her own iconoclastic self?

Third, two major concerns about Ruether's methodological construction in the prophetic-liberating tradition in the Bible are noted. The first concerns her claim that the prophetic tradition is central to the Bible. It leads to certain related questions: for example, on what grounds does she reject other traditions, such as covenant, as the central tradition? Or, though her claim of prophetic tradition is grounded on biblical scholarship, do most Scripture scholars take to mean the tradition in the same way as she does?

The second concern is raised by several feminist theologians who are concerned about the prophetic-liberating tradition itself. Elisabeth Schüssler Fiorenza criticizes her for idealizing the prophetic tradition and failing to identify the androcentric elements within the tradition.[50] She thus concludes that Ruether's approach "serves more to rescue biblical religion from its feminist critics than to develop a feminist historical hermeneutics."[51]

Other feminist theologians echo Fiorenza's criticism and point out some problematic aspects of prophetic traditions: "[they] are themselves part of an oppressive patriarchal theology and not themselves adequate models for feminist theology."[52] Siker observes that Rebecca Chopp, a former student of Ruether, further criticizes that the prophetic-liberating tradition lacks historical accuracy and the ability to identify practices of subversion and transformation that already exist. Critics thus wonder if Ruether has elevated the prophetic principle into an ideology itself. I find these criticisms and questions both challenging and, yet, necessary.

As a whole, we can draw upon these concerns raised by her feminist colleagues and comment that Ruether, while overtly trying to counteract patriarchy in the Bible, still misses recognizing those androcentric elements in the texts she employed and the problem of the prophetic tradition she proposed. Methodologically speaking, it points to the question of her exegetical accuracy and how well she has achieved it in her reading of the prophetic texts.

However, we still have to acknowledge that her feminist interpretation is rather impressive, partly because at times she turns to the expertise of biblical scholars for insight, as in the case of Gutiérrez. Concrete instances include the interpretation of

Genesis 1:27 ("*imago*") in which Ruether first consults Hebrew Scripture scholars before making her claim that "dominion over creation is the essential meaning of the term 'image' in this text,"[53] and that "the expression 'male and female' is not intended to modify the phrase 'image of God.'"[54]

In conclusion, although there are mixed comments regarding her approach to and use of Scripture, I agree with Siker that Ruether's attempt uncovers those "fossilized texts" and "fossilized interpretations" in the Bible, and, hence, calls for honest reflection on how and why the Bible is used as it is in the Church, especially in the field of ethics.

William C. Spohn[55]

The approach of William Spohn (1944–2005) toward ethics was basically one of virtue ethics. He believed that "virtue ethics provides the most comprehensive account of moral experience."[56] However, Spohn was also convinced that virtue ethics in turn provides the most appropriate avenue for engaging Scripture.[57] Therefore, our discussion will focus on his engagement with Scripture in ethics rather than solely on the use of Scripture.

For Spohn the Bible as a whole is the story of a people called and led by God to be a distinctive community and, individually, a particular sort of person. It presents a new way of life that is inseparable from the history that has revealed God. Thus, the use of Scripture in Christian ethics must be rooted in this history. With regards to its authority, he claimed that "Scripture has authority over discernment but not the final word."[58] Still, the other three indispensible sources "at least must be compatible with the basic patterns inherent in the story of Jesus," for the story of Jesus emphasizes certain moral dispositions that other sources neglect (e.g., the forgiveness of enemies).[59] That said, he acknowledged that any coherent ethical argument must draw on these other sources in an integrated way.

John Donahue notes that "go and do likewise" (Luke 10:37) and "only, live your life in a manner worthy of the gospel" (Phil

1:27) are the two most crucial biblical texts in guiding Spohn's constructive work. Still, Spohn employed other New Testament texts, with special attention to the story of Jesus. Among the Old Testament writings, he mainly quoted the Psalms and Isaiah.

Spohn, himself, commented that the particular focus on Jesus has various reasons:[60] the trend within the field of New Testament ethics; his view that the New Testament represents a way of life (i.e., pattern of discipleship) through the story of Jesus; and his perception of Jesus in this story as "normative for Christian ethics as its concrete universal."[61] In other words, Jesus is the paradigm that guides Christian living in a normative way.

Spohn's overall engagement with Scripture takes various forms. First, he moved away from the traditional emphasis on history and paid attention to the different literary genres and the contexts of the texts. He focused particularly on biblical narratives and pointed out that they guide moral reflection and action more directly than other literary forms in several ways.[62] For instance, biblical narratives interpreted in faith communities can inform and inspire moral dispositions/virtues (e.g., the narrative of the woman caught in adultery in John 8:1–11 informs us of the call for both justice and mercy). As a whole, Spohn was convinced that narrative theology "operates closer to the fabric of Christian moral experience than most speculative theologies...[and] can support a broader definition of ethics that recognizes the normative guidance that symbolic material brings to disposition and character."[63]

Second, Spohn highlighted the paradigmatic role of certain themes and texts in the Bible in transforming one's character with respect to perception, dispositions, and identity. For example, the Sermon on the Mount in Matthew 5–7 corrects and sharpens our perception regarding fairness/justice and intercessory prayer; instructs our emotions to form deeper dispositions that allow us to conform our lives to the pattern of Jesus' life, and highlights our Christian identity as one of a forgiving community.

Third, Spohn engaged in the provision of directives for using Scripture for moral discourse. By comparing the exodus narrative and the story of the holy war (in Judges), for instance, Spohn demonstrated, among other things, that the image of God as healing judge (rather than dispenser of retributive justice) is appropriate to our situation, and the corresponding action concurs with the standards of human morality.

Spohn dealt with the task of hermeneutics and its problem in the revised edition of his *What Are They Saying about Scripture and Ethics?*[64] He realized that hermeneutics has become central to the use of Scripture and, thus, proposed a three-step framework that analyzes ethical arguments that appeal to Scripture: the selection, interpretation, and application of the selected texts.

Famously, in this book, he identified five different models of using Scripture.[65] Among them, he perceived the "responding love" model as the most constructive approach: it supplements other approaches and "builds on the work of the narrative theologians but broadens the selection beyond story to include biblical symbols, mandates, and terms of address for God."[66] It understands that one is called not just to imitate the master but to participate in the life and mission of Jesus Christ.

Nevertheless, his hermeneutical approach is also one of "appreciation"—through which the gap between Scripture's world and ours can be bridged. This points to the cultivation of "analogical imagination."[67] Analogy attends to the relationship between "the biblical text in relation to its world and today's Christian community in relation to its world."[68] For Spohn, the story of Jesus is the prime "analogate" that guides our Christian imagination. This analogical imagination discerns those paradigms and guiding images that connect the biblical story with our own situation so that they shape our action in such a way that we "go and do likewise" what Jesus said and did. Moreover, through faithful imagination, the story of Jesus, in turn, becomes "paradigmatic for moral perception, disposition, and identity...[for] it enables us to recognize *which* features of experience are significant, guides *how* we act, and forms *who* we are in the community of faith."[69] In the story of Zacchaeus (Luke 19:1–10), for instance, the story captures "the pattern of the Christian moral life as a response to the surprising and undeserved gift of God's acceptance of us."[70] Creative imagination then allows us to identify in Zacchaeus our own experience of lacking the power to do what is right.

In short, analogical imagination reveals to each of us in a unique way what Christ's invitation to discipleship is. The challenge of Christian ethics today is thus to think analogically—to be faithful and creative at the same time.

As a whole, Spohn's effort in proposing an integral task for a Christian ethics informed by Scripture has drawn positive attention from both areas of theology. Among Christian ethicists, Martha Stortz was impressed by his attempt to bring Scripture "to bear on issues that had previously been treated within the narrow scope of moral norms and casuistry."[71] Michael Cartwright also commended him for challenging Christian ethicists to go beyond the descriptive results found in biblical scholarship to explain the moral and spiritual meaning of imitating Jesus. His methodological approach likewise received warm welcome. James Bretzke even commented that the use of the concept of analogy is the most appropriate way to engage the reader and Scripture.[72]

Biblical scholars Hays and Matera praised Spohn for highlighting the importance of biblical narratives for the moral life of believers. Yet, they also rightly expressed their concerns about his actual use of Scripture. First, Spohn did not deal more fully with the gospel narratives. Second, Spohn seemed not to take sufficient account of the apocalyptic element of the Gospels and the diversity of the New Testament writings. I also agree that Spohn could use and discuss the Pauline and Pastoral Epistles more (e.g., those other Pauline texts that may condone a male-dominated structure of marriage) for it is in them that much of our spiritual and moral tradition is rooted.[73] Therefore, like the other above-surveyed ethicists, he seemed to remain silent about those problematic texts and/or unable to confront them.

Nevertheless, these biblical scholars praise Spohn's work for being well informed by contemporary biblical studies. For example, his discussion of Jesus' kingdom message is noticeably influenced by the work of New Testament scholar Nicholas Thomas Wright.

In sum, I think Donahue's remarks after Spohn's death can best summarize Spohn's commitment and contribution to

Scripture and ethics: "Bill provided a guide to Catholic theology for the then largely unexplored territory of Scripture and moral theology."[74]

Like the situation we have seen among the biblical scholars, each of the ethicists examined has offered certain specific methodological insights into the use of Scripture in ethics. First, they have demonstrated that there is a real need to interact with both the texts and biblical scholarship. Second, the task of hermeneutics is necessary not only for bridging the two disciplines but also in the actual use of Scripture. Specifically, one's ethical framework is crucial to how the biblical texts are used and interpreted. The attempts of these ethicists somehow reveal a stronger interest in integrating Scripture into their ethical framework than biblical scholars show about the ethical theory of ethicists. Third, their employment of Scripture in ethics confirms the development and shift from concern with norms and biblical authority to the role of Scripture in forming vision/values and practices of communities of discipleship and its relevance in equality and social justice.

However, certain issues regarding the selection, textual interpretation, and methodology also emerged. In the first place, the biblical texts employed are, in general, very selective. They tend to be limited to certain traditions or themes perceived by the ethicists as helpful in advocating their particular agenda. Thus, these ethicists' use of Scripture, though it goes beyond the proof-texting model, remains problematic.

Second, when some of these ethicists interact with biblical scholarship and even attempt to engage in the task of exegesis, the overall performance is unsatisfactory, either in terms of quantity or quality. They have, moreover, interacted with biblical scholars in a minimal, selective manner.

These two points (selective use and insufficient exegesis) lead to a related and, yet, important issue—the approach toward problematic or "bad" texts, that is, those texts that contradict outright the claims of the author. All these four ethicists fail to deal with these texts, either by avoidance during the process of selection or by not engaging them exegetically (and carefully). This issue, I think, deserves some attention here.

On the one hand, some ethicists have shown that it is not impossible to handle and confront these problematic texts. Fiorenza, for example, employs a feminist critical evaluative hermeneutics to challenge androcentric constructions in those androcentric texts (e.g., Col 3:18–25) and critically analyzes them. She concludes that the early Christian ethos of co-equal discipleship in community can equally claim scriptural authority and canonicity just as the patriarchal pattern of submission has done.[75]

On the other hand, biblical scholars also show us that it is through careful exegesis alone that we can know whether a text is problematic. For instance, Harrington and George Smiga treat, in detail, those possible problematic passages in the four Gospels that seem anti-Jewish (e.g., Matt 23:13–36; John 8:44). They show us that by placing the Gospels in their original Jewish contexts, one will understand that the Gospels are not anti-Jewish, and those seemingly problematic texts may only have an anti-Jewish potential.[76]

Third, as a whole, when these scholars employ Scripture in their ethical reflection, they are still concerned more about interpreting the text's meaning for the contemporary world than with first examining its original meaning to see if the text can be rightly employed. In other words, they are still more interested in ethical hermeneutics than in first understanding the text.

In these two reviews of the development of an integrated Scripture-based ethics, we note that both biblical scholars and theological ethicists have either stressed more the importance of the scriptural text or the importance of ethical hermeneutics. This observation struck me as revealing: a balanced view that understanding the scriptural text and ethical hermeneutics are equally important seems to be the right direction toward constructing a more integrated scriptural ethics.

CHAPTER THREE

MOVING TOWARD A CONSENSUS

The Equal Importance of the Scriptural Text and of Ethical Hermeneutics

We note from the previous two chapters that the past twenty years or so have witnessed positive developments within the two disciplines to construct an integrated Scripture-based ethics. These developments, however, reveal two contrasting realities. On the one hand, a more integrated Scripture-based ethics has not been achieved: both biblical scholars and theological ethicists have either stressed the importance of the scriptural text or the importance of ethical hermeneutics. In other words, there is a lack of balance among these scholars in their corresponding approaches.

On the other hand, they point us in the right direction of what doing biblical ethics can be: it would take the Bible seriously and build its findings upon a sound ethical theory or hermeneutics. Among most recent scholars committed to this goal, I note that New Testament scholar Richard Burridge and Christian ethicist Allen Verhey have tried to maintain such a balance in their writings.

Richard A. Burridge[1]

Richard Burridge is an Anglican priest and professor of New Testament in England. Because of his former academic training in the Classics, Burridge is particularly interested in exploring the literary genre of the Gospels. Specifically, he is known for advocating the view that the genre of the Gospels is one of ancient biography.

In *What Are the Gospels? A Comparison with Graeco-Roman Biography*, Burridge examines the four Gospels in light of features that serve as methodological criteria for examining ancient biographies —namely, opening features (e.g., title), subject, external features (e.g., size/scale), and internal features (e.g., attitude/values). He corrects and builds upon the earlier attempts to understand the Gospels as biography, and emphasizes that, as a genre, biography or biographical narrative (*βίος*) is a flexible, diverse genre that "nestles among neighboring genres such as historiography, rhetoric... and the novel."[2] As a result, he is convinced that, contrary to the mainstream view that the Gospels are sui generis, the four Gospels have, in fact, many features in common with *βίοι* and, thus, belong to the overall genre of ancient Graeco-Roman *βίοι*.

Commentators, in general, agree that Burridge has made his case in defending the biographical character of the Gospels. However, I find its subsequent implications for New Testament studies equally significant. The first concerns the issue of hermeneutics: Burridge insists that genre plays a significant role in the interpretation of the texts. Thus, the diverse, flexible nature of *βίος* implies a flexible interpretation of the Gospels in which one finds various materials, such as didactic, apologetic, and polemic materials (and purposes).

A second and subsequent implication is that the key to the interpretation of the text is the *subject* of the narrative. This is because a biographical interpretation of the texts invites us to focus on the subject. In the four Gospels, Jesus of Nazareth becomes the key to interpretation. Hence, a flexible interpretation of the narratives of Jesus would imply that it is not limited to an interpretation of the historical facts of Jesus of Nazareth but is also open to a theological interpretation of the subject. The Gospels become "Christology in narrative form."

A third implication of the biographical hypothesis concerns the social setting and function of the Gospels. Burridge points out that the biographical approach offers "a critique of too much community-based sociological analysis of the gospel audiences."[3]

As *βίοι*, the Gospels are not written specifically for the hypothetical community that produced them but for a more general audience and with diverse social functions (e.g., apologetic and polemic purposes). Their publication and delivery is likewise intended for other groups across a broad geographical area.[4] As a result, viewing the Gospels as *βίοι* can "liberate us from the circularity of deducing the communities from the text and then interpreting the text in light of these (deduced) communities."[5]

Last but not least, ancient biographies "held together both words and deeds in portraying their central subject."[6] What is central to this genre is the emphasis that the words and deeds of the subject are inseparable. One cannot attend to the words alone or vice versa. Thus, a biographical approach to the Gospels does not perceive the texts as merely a collection of sayings by Jesus but that Jesus' narrated teachings are inseparable from his narrated deeds. Specifically, both his words and deeds are part of his proclamation of the kingdom of God.

All these implications are applicable to the study of New Testament ethics as well. A comprehensive and systematic study of New Testament ethics rooted in the biographical hypothesis is found in his recent major book, *Imitating Jesus: An Inclusive Approach to New Testament Ethics*, and in a related article written in the same year.[7] This major work is generally an expansion of what he pursued in *What Are the Gospels?* It "looks at how New Testament ethics should be interpreted in the light of [the] argument that the gospels are essentially biographies of Jesus, using South African apartheid as a case study."[8]

The overall aim of *Imitating Jesus* is to offer an alternative approach to New Testament ethics. Burridge is worried that New Testament ethics today is still done in a way that overemphasizes the rigorous ethical teachings of Jesus, and the example of Jesus is either ignored or treated inadequately.[9] Moreover, he is concerned that "the vast majority of works on New Testament ethics concentrate almost exclusively on the ethical material within the New Testament; any attempt to relate it to today may include a brief consideration of the problems in so doing and of possible methodologies, but little by way of actual content or application."[10] Thus, he also aims at promoting the pragmatic task as Hays has done.

His approach to New Testament ethics, therefore, is biographical. He is convinced that the literary genre is crucial to the interpretation of the texts. He claims that "[i]n order to be [b]iblical, we have to interpret the gospels according to this [ancient biographical] genre."[11] This methodological claim has certain implications for our study of New Testament ethics. First, as mentioned above, a biographical reading of the texts would emphasize that the subject's words are inseparable from one's actual deeds, for the narrative of the subject's deeds provides the context for the sayings. In the context of New Testament ethics, therefore, it means that focusing on the sayings of Jesus alone is inadequate. Rather, one must set Jesus' ethical teaching within the context of the narrative that portrays his deeds. For instance, the rigorous and demanding Sermon on the Mount must be interpreted in the context of Jesus' radical loving acceptance of others. Though the process of interpreting Jesus' words and deeds is a complex one, and creates a tension between radical moral teachings and radical love, it should be the starting point.

Second, ancient biographies were often written to offer a portrait of the subject. Burridge explains, "the ancients wanted to depict the subject's character with a portrait of them through a combination of their deeds and words, through anecdotes and stories as much as their sayings or speeches…often it will also reveal something further about the person's life, or bring the author's major themes to a climax."[12] Thus, within the context of New Testament ethics, it points to the person of Jesus as the locus and the starting point of our ethical reflection. For Burridge, the New Testament is "not an ethical manual, nor is it just about providing moral instructions; instead, it challenges the reader with its central Christological claim and the consequent call to follow Jesus in discipleship."[13] Therefore, Christology is the key to ethical hermeneutics, and the study of New Testament ethics should focus on and begin with the ethics of Jesus.

The depiction of the subject's character by means of biographical narratives leads us to a third ethical proposition: the practice of imitation and of appropriating the subject's virtues. Ancient biographies were written to provide an example for others to follow. This idea of imitation is not unlike the Jewish *ma'aseh* (precedence) where "the disciple is expected to observe and imitate his master as a way of imitating Torah and ultimately becoming holy as God is holy."[14] Therefore, the New Testament canon should be interpreted as biographical narratives that include ethics, which help followers to imitate Jesus. In this way, "imitating Jesus" is the core theme of the New Testament ethics.

The fourth proposition is built around the previous outcomes. The New Testament canon invites us to imitate Jesus' radical loving acceptance of all people within an open and inclusive community. That means, the New Testament needs to be interpreted within an inclusive community. In fact, this inclusive approach is already hinted at the subtitle of his book.

In *Imitating Jesus*, Burridge first presents and discusses the ethical contents and themes of the New Testament in chronological order. What follows is the application of his inclusive approach to New Testament ethics—he discusses the debate of apartheid in South Africa and interprets the Bible through the lenses of "the imitation of Jesus" and of "an open, inclusive community."

In discussing each of the New Testament writings, Burridge basically follows a particular structure that focuses on the abovementioned propositions. He begins with certain Christological claims, followed by a discussion of the Law and love, and, then, identifies the ethical issues presented in the texts, and concludes with reflections on the meaning of imitating Jesus.

In the exploration of the ethics of (the historical) Jesus, for example, Burridge first clarifies that the Gospels do not depict Jesus as just a teacher of morality. Rather, the proclamation of the reign of God is crucial to Jesus' ethical teaching (Mark 1:14). Jesus' ethics is one of response to the proclamation—he calls us to repentance and discipleship (Mark 1:15–20; Matt 4:18–22). Therefore, Jesus' ethical teaching is "not a separate body of moral instructions, but rather part of his preaching of the eschatological in-breaking of the reign of God, which demands a total and immediate response from his hearers."[15] Although those specific ethical teachings are rigorous and all-demanding, they aim at intensifying what the Law demands with an ethics of self-denial and renunciation. The heart of Jesus' teaching is still the double commandment of love.

From there, Burridge examines Jesus' attitude and actions toward sinners (e.g., his encounter with Zacchaeus in Luke 19:1–10), and concludes that Jesus' deeds and examples of open acceptance of all are coherent with his strenuous commands. We are called to imitate Jesus' merciful and loving acceptance of all, and our individual responses must be situated in the context of a new community of disciples.

Regarding the ethics of Paul, even though the genre of Pauline letters is not biographical narrative *per se*, the letters can still be interpreted in a similar manner, for Paul bases everything on the "Jesus event." Thus, by examining Paul's theology and those contextual ethical imperatives (e.g., household codes), Burridge claims that Paul's ethics "is still supremely an ethics of response, even though the preaching of the kingdom has become the event of the King, with Christology being absolutely central for both Paul's own new life and for his theology and ethics."[16] The theme of imitation of Jesus' inclusive love is found in Paul's writings too: Paul constantly appeals to his readers to imitate him as he imitated Christ (1 Cor 11:1). Specifically, they are not just to be humble and self-giving but also to bear the failings of the weak and to welcome them into the community (Rom 15:1–13). Thus, Paul's ethics shares the same basic outline as that of Jesus, and one should read Paul "as following the creative complementarity of Jesus' rigorous and demanding ethics together with his acceptance of sinners within his community."[17]

In the case of the ethics found in the four Gospels, each of the four evangelists basically attempts to tell the story of Jesus "in such a way that readers will imitate his life in response."[18] Still, Burridge recognizes the different ethical emphases by each of the Gospel writers: Mark's Christology and understanding of the law and love points to the interim eschatological ethics in suffering. The ethics of discipleship emphasized by Mark means following

Jesus wholeheartedly, forming an open and inclusive community, and imitating Jesus to be friend of sinners (e.g., 1:16–20; 3:13–19).

For Matthew, Jesus is the new Moses and true righteous interpreter of the Law (Matt 23). Jesus' words and deeds reveal that righteousness within the reign of God is central to his ethical teachings (chapter 13). Imitating the Matthean Jesus means learning to be teachers of the new righteousness (i.e., not based on the Law but on Jesus Christ) within an inclusive community of forgiving love.

For Luke, Jesus' universal mission is for all people, with special concerns for the disadvantaged. As a result, both the words and deeds of Jesus as narrated by Luke point to the concrete needs to care for the marginalized, as found in Jesus' inaugural speech in Nazareth (4:16–21), and his association with sinners and encounter with women (e.g., 7:33–50). Imitating the Lucan Jesus, therefore, means being friends of the marginalized and of sinners, and forming an inclusive community that embraces people of all paths.

For Burridge, John's rich narrative of Jesus has, contrary to the common view, many ethical implications about following and imitating Jesus. The absence of a specific ethical command is simply because "everything is now subordinated under the 'new commandment' to love one another as he has loved us."[19] Finally, the call to imitate Jesus refers to following his self-sacrificial love within a mixed inclusive community.

In the final chapter, Burridge applies his biographical approach to analyze how the New Testament should be interpreted in the debate of apartheid in South Africa. In other words, he engages in ethical hermeneutics on a particular locality and its specific practice. He first analyzes the use of Scripture by both sides of the apartheid debate (i.e., the proponents and the critics) to support (or to critique) apartheid. He concludes that none of the approaches employed by either side (i.e., by looking for rules/commands, principles/universal values, paradigms/examples, and symbolic worldview) could avoid abuse. He thus proposes the use of the biographical approach of which the imitation of Jesus is the ethical hermeneutical key. Only by imitating Jesus' words and deeds, and reading Scripture together within the context of an open and inclusive community, are we able to apply the moral teaching of the New Testament to the case of apartheid. Here, a contextual reading would emphasize the inclusion of the dissident voices of the South Africans by the community. Consequently, such a reading would judge that the pro-apartheid theology fails to imitate Jesus by not hearing and responding to the voice of South Africa's oppressed.

As a whole, Burridge identifies a consistent pattern in the historical Jesus' life and teachings: Jesus proposes a rigorous moral teaching that is grounded in the commandment of love and forms a mixed, inclusive community that responds to his demanding teachings by means of imitation.[20] In this way, our understanding of the New Testament ethics through the lens of biography must consider the overall depiction of Jesus' life, teaching, and practices. And the unity of New Testament ethics subsequently lies in the core theme of imitation. Specifically, the disciples are to imitate Jesus by forming open and inclusive communities.

Many welcome Burridge's *Imitating Jesus* as a constructive, comprehensive, unique, and important book about New Testament studies and New Testament ethics. They praise him for engaging in dialogue with New Testament scholarship (of both the past and the current) and other perspectives, such as feminism and Judaism, in his enquiry. He also engages in literature normally employed by ethicists (especially in his case study of apartheid). In addition, some commend him for presenting the materials in a nontechnical way that can benefit theological ethicists who are interested in Scripture-based ethics. However, many note that the work does not contain enough exegetical materials (as would be expected from a biblical scholar) and, hence, it is basically a presentation of mainstream biblical scholarship. This implies that he does not engage in direct interpretation of the texts but simply summarizes the views of other scholars.

Regarding the content of his work, moreover, it is obvious that Burridge does not treat all the New Testament writings, such as the Catholic Epistles and the book of Revelation. Several commentators are rightly concerned that he does not present the entire New Testament ethics but only the ethics of the four Gospels and of Paul. This leads Hays and others to wonder if the omission is due to the fact that these writings do not have biographical narrative or do not support an inclusive ethics. Moreover, Burridge does not seem to offer concrete answers except for some general exhortations to the contemporary ethical questions he raised. It gives the impression that while he rightly urges us to interpret the biblical text in a biographical and inclusive approach, he does not state clearly enough how to achieve the goal. One reviewer further notes that he does not clarify the issue of diversity within a unified New Testament ethics either.[21] In addition, I agree that Burridge, at times, takes the positions of his colleagues for his own and, hence, does not offer many new insights in terms of ethical content. For instance, he basically follows the general understanding among scholars (e.g., Schrage, Hays, and Matera) that Paul's ethics is grounded in his Christology. The idea that Jesus is a model for moral response is, likewise, already discussed by Matera and Hays. The only difference is that he sees New Testament ethics grounded in Christology more than other previously discussed biblical scholars do.

Despite these particular concerns regarding the content of his work, Burridge's methodology and approach to the interpretation of the texts has drawn positive comments. Specifically, his inclusive approach is similar to, and, hence, can benefit from, those who advocate a contextual reading of the texts in that it attends to the cultural circumstances of the communities. An inclusive approach as such also avoids those limitations attributed to feminist and liberation theologians whose approaches risk the exclusion of certain groups.

Furthermore, his approach challenges those who find ethical import only from the words of Jesus. And Burridge not only demonstrates the "how to" (as Hays does) but also challenges biblical scholars to go beyond the exegetical task to consider contemporary applications. In the case study of the apartheid situation in South Africa, for instance, he turns to the literature of Christian ethics in order to offer guidance in constructive application of Scripture to the problem.

Still, some scholars find his approach too narrow, one that leads to a reductionistic treatment of the genre of the Gospels into biography alone. Although the Gospels share many features with ancient Graeco-Roman *βίοι*, there are also certain features unique to the New Testament that are not explored or integrated into the argument. In addition, the emphasis on inclusiveness has several practical obstacles: commentators who raise this issue are rightly concerned about whether there should be limits to such an inclusive community; and if so, one needs to know when and how to exclude.[22] Although Burridge acknowledges the existence and challenges of these limits, he does not provide much practical information on how the community could be maintained and how its "inclusive selection" is determined. One reviewer further raises the concern that "even inclusive communities will find ways to mess up the reading of scripture."[23] Thus, one wonders if such emphasis is too loose a category for theological ethics.

Despite these criticisms and concerns, Burridge's work as a whole demonstrates that a biographical genre could make a significant difference in the interpretation of the New Testament canon, especially in the area of New Testament ethics. The ethical implications emerging from a biographical reading of the texts reveal that such an approach is not simply a method/genre within literary criticisms. Its emphases on imitating Jesus, on forming open, inclusive communities, and on the person of Jesus (on both his words and deeds) and Christology as the key to ethical hermeneutics provide a solid platform for ethical analysis—as a concrete platform for ethical analysis it goes beyond narrative ethics or character ethics that focuses either on narratives or the community's formation alone.[24] In fact, a biographical, inclusive approach can be seen as a sum of these ethical theories and bears a trait of virtue ethics. As will be explored in the next chapter, these emphases—especially the focus on the person as exemplar, the call to imitation, the insistence on the community and its formation, and the goal of becoming an inclusive faith community—are closely related to the structure of virtue ethics and the various dimensions of virtues, which entail character, practices, exemplar, and communal identity.

In his forthcoming book, *Money, Sex, Power, Violence and the Meaning of Life: Following Jesus Today*, Burridge likewise emphasizes the importance of applying the findings of textual interpretation to today's pragmatic issues. In doing so, he refines the fourfold method of Hays—the descriptive, canonical, interpretative, and practical stages—and, from there, treats five transcultural human moral experiences—money, sex, power, violence, and the meaning of life—based on the core message of imitation and inclusive community.

Therefore, Burridge's work gives us a hint, from the perspective of biblical scholarship, of what a more balanced and integrated Scripture-based ethics can be: it embraces the importance of ethical hermeneutics while paying attention to the importance of the text. And in doing so, we can build our findings upon a sound platform of ethical analysis or ethical theory/hermeneutics. To conclude my description of his contribution in constructing a more integrated Scripture-based ethics, I quote Matera's words that I think appropriate: "[It is] one of those rare studies that moves the discipline forward."[25]

Allen Verhey[26]

Allen Verhey, a Dutch Reformed (Calvinist) Christian ethicist, is known as a prolific writer. Although many of his more recent publications are focused on medical ethics (and bioethics), Verhey has addressed a variety of topics, ranging from anthropology to communal discernment, from Calvinism to Scripture.[27]

However, there is a common feature among these writings: the employment of Scripture in theological reflections, especially on the applications of Christian ethics. Verhey states that he is particularly interested in the relation of Scripture and Christian ethics. His first major work in exploring this relation is his dissertation that analyzed Walter Rauschenbusch's use of Scripture as a case for understanding the reasons for the diversity of uses.[28] In subsequent years, he continued to survey contemporary methodological resources for relating Scripture and ethics, as well as turn to the Bible for insights on certain ethical issues. For instance, he explores the issues of assisted suicide and euthanasia by turning to his particular tradition and by interpreting Judas's suicide in Matthew 27:3–10.

Later in his book *Reading the Bible in the Strange World of Medicine,* he similarly demonstrates his application of Scripture to other medical, bioethical issues, such as abortion and genetic interventions. As Andrew Lustig comments, Verhey "rejects simplistic readings of either Scripture or these difficult issues and instead explores, with a rich blend of insight, analysis, and exhortation, how attending to Scripture can challenge the 'strange' ethos of modern medicine."[29] In his latest book on ethics, *The Christian Art of Dying: Learning from Jesus,* Verhey again turns to the Bible—the biblical accounts of Jesus' death in particular—as a paradigm for his reflection on dying well. From there, he explicitly identifies and discusses certain needed Christian virtues, such as patience and courage, and practices like mourning and comforting and praying. In *Nature and Altering It,* Verhey similarly demonstrates that the biblical narrative can be an alternative source for understanding our nature and reflecting upon contemporary moral issues, such as ecological and political discourses.[30]

All these examples reveal his confidence and ability to deal with scriptural texts. Indeed, his knowledge of Scripture and its interpretation has been well received by Scripture scholars and biblical theologians, and some even recognize him as a New Testament scholar.[31] Concrete evidence of this is his widely read earlier work on New Testament ethics, *The Great Reversal: Ethics of the New Testament* (1984) within the Protestant circles. Even Catholic scholars like Donald Senior and Lisa Sowle Cahill are amazed by his command of biblical materials and exegetical skill.[32] Moreover, his major work, *Remembering Jesus: Christian Community, Scripture, and the Moral Life,* has drawn fuller attention from the academia (especially within the Roman Catholic tradition). Some perceive this work as a development and fulfillment of the insights of his 1984 study.

Furthermore, between the publications of these two books, Verhey developed a specific approach of doing Scripture-based ethics. It emphasizes the need of remembering Jesus, the role of the community, as well as the importance of practices and performances. I turn now to his publications to explicate, in two steps, his model of Scripture-based ethics. First, I will look at his work as a biblical theologian in doing New Testament ethics. Second, I explore his work as an ethicist, that is, his use of Scripture in Christian ethics.

Verhey as a Biblical Theologian

Verhey's talent as a biblical theologian is best demonstrated in his *The Great Reversal*. In this work, he aims at bridging the gulf that separates New Testament studies and Christian ethics from each other and from the life of the Christian community. He is convinced that only when the gulf is bridged will New Testament ethics be able to address the issues concerning the continuing Church. In so doing, Verhey constructs the bridge from the side of the New Testament—that is, from the perspective of biblical scholarship. Therefore, in the first three chapters of this book, he presents a standard, chronological, descriptive study of the moral teachings of the New Testament. He begins with the ethics of the historical Jesus, then moves on to the ethics of the early Church remembering Jesus, and finally to the ethics of the New Testament writers (in canonical sequence). He then surveys certain methodological problems and resources for relating Scripture and contemporary ethics and offers his own proposal for the use of Scripture in Christian ethics.

Verhey's subsequent construal of the ethics of Jesus (which seems to be centered on Mark) is grounded in Jesus' turning of the apocalyptic expectation of a "great reversal" into one that brings transformation of values and good news to the poor. These reversed values include humility, confidence in God, and generosity. The ethics of the early Church in remembering Jesus and expecting his return, however, result from the tradition that preserved and shaped the memory of the words and deeds of Jesus, and the paraenetic tradition developed and handed down alongside. Verhey notes that there are diverse ethical emphases among the various forms of traditions and claims that the purpose of these different traditions is not merely for moral education but "to encourage and exhort Christians to the new life given and demanded by what God has done in Jesus Christ."[33]

Nevertheless, these diverse ethical contents address various communities and their moral problems: Mark presents a heroic morality; Matthew calls for a surpassing righteousness; Luke presents an ethics of care and respect; and Paul urges Christians to discern a life that is appropriate to the new age. They all converge into "loyalty to the risen Lord"—who is remembered, whose words and deeds are taken as to be normative, and who continues to guide and speak to his faithful followers.

Here, I find his understanding of the Sermon on the Mount in Matthew 5–7, especially his view on the Beatitudes, noteworthy for it gives hints of the kind of ethical approach he has in mind for his own proposal—one that emphasizes character formation and virtues: "Matthew 'ethicizes' the tradition so that the emphasis falls on the exhortation to develop certain character traits in response to Jesus' proclamation of the kingdom...With the beatitudes that Matthew adds, these constitute a catalogue of virtues."[34]

After surveying certain methodological problems and resources for relating Scripture and contemporary ethics, Verhey turns to his proposal that would "license the movement [in argument] from the New Testament to claims about the reality within which we must respond, to claims about our moral identity as people loyal to God, and to claims about the dispositions and intentions that mark truthfulness to that reality and integrity with that identity."[35]

This proposal further makes clear the kind of ethical model Verhey undertakes: one that attends to the context, moral identity, and subsequent practices and dispositions. The commandment of giving up one's possessions (Mark 10:29), for example, is "[a] statement of a moral posture that is freed from bondage to possessions for the practice of generosity and hospitality."[36] The use of Scripture is valid only when one admits the continuous authority of Jesus Christ to reveal God's Word to the Christian community in its moral discernment.

Many reviewers praise Verhey for combining the knowledge of New Testament criticism and contemporary methods of moral theology and moral philosophy in this work. He pays close attention to the biblical texts and deals with them in detail and judiciously. His description of the New Testament's ethics, however, is not without critics. One reviewer, in particular, judges his overall exegetical work as "pedestrian"—there is inadequate engagement with current biblical scholarship and he scarcely resolves exegetical impasses.[37]

Despite this criticism, I identify two related insights of Verhey's effort that can be helpful to our search for a more integrated Scripture-based ethics. First, Verhey reveals that, even as Christian ethicists, we have to take the biblical texts seriously and pay attention to the original meanings of these texts prior to employing them in our ethical reflections. Second, Verhey demonstrates that such a task is *possible*. While it is important to listen to what Scripture scholars say regarding the texts, Christian ethicists also need to take courage to step out from their own field into the biblical world. Verhey leads us—Christian ethicists in particular—to understand the importance of exegeting the text for Scripture-based ethics by his very own example.

Verhey as a Christian Ethicist

Verhey generally adapts MacIntyre's seminal notion of practice as a core element of his ethical framework. For instance, in his treatment of the problem of scarcity of medical resources, he identifies truthfulness, humility, justice, gratitude, compassion, and care as important standards of excellence, practices, and virtues for the formation of good policy. Some ethicists thus perceive him as a virtue ethicist and put him alongside Stanley Hauerwas and John Howard Yoder in building a virtue model of Christian ethics. Although Verhey puts more emphasis on practice than virtue itself and understands Christian ethics as primarily a matter of communal practice, I would understand him as a virtue ethicist, at least in a broad sense. It is because, as will be discussed in the next chapter, both practices and communal identity are important dimensions of virtue. Moreover, when he claims that practices, rather than choices, characterize the community, his view bears a trait of character ethics: as the Word of God, Scripture not only plays the role of revealer but also of sanctifier through which God "renews life, transforms identities, and recreates and resurrects humankind."[38]

Here, Verhey is convinced that Scripture is an authority for the Church's faith and life, especially for its moral discourse and judgment. He further points out that Scripture has authority in the very notion of Church, for it is "the confession of the believing community and of the members of that community that their submission to God and to the cause of God will be guided and tested by attention to these writings."[39] One particular way that the Bible exercises its authority is through the practice of reading Scripture in a community. This understanding has three related ethical implications.

First, by retrieving Gustafson's understanding of the Church as a community of interpretation and action, Verhey underscores the importance of practices and performances of Scripture—which include praying, reading Scripture, and the practice of moral discourse—by particular communities. Second, it calls for greater attention given to community and context. How Scripture is used in ethical reflection depends on the context of the religious community within which the authority of Scripture is experienced.[40] Within the Church community, Scripture and the Church are correlative concepts: Scripture is the book of the Church and, thus, would not exist without the Church, while the Church preserves its identity and character and reforms its common life with the help of Scripture. Third, the practice of reading Scripture in Christian community helps remembering the Lord and cultivates certain standards of excellence, such as fidelity, creativity, discipline, and discernment. It is also a practice of piety. Of course, the text must be read in light of the whole and as a continuing story.

This Reformed view thus understands Scripture as the best resource for the constant renewal of the Church's life. However, Verhey notes that the use of sources other than Scripture—such as natural science, natural morality, and human experiences—is necessary in Christian ethics. Furthermore, Verhey understands that Christian ethics takes on its task of renewing the community "by way of reminder" (Rom 15:15). In simple terms, it means remembering and telling the good news of God. It is upon this understanding that Verhey constructs his hermeneutic of remembering and use of Scripture.

Verhey acknowledges that the use of remembrance had been found and used in Greek and Hebrew writings with such terms as *anamnesis* and *zakhar*, respectively. And his emphasis on remembering can be traced back to one of Gustafson's four aspects of internalization of Scripture emerging from a communal hermeneutic:

> The third aspect of internalization is "memory," and Christian churches are communities of memory. The Bible tells the story of Israel, Christ, and the church, and that story is internalized, owned as 'our' story, in the continuing church...[It] is not the only 'object' to bear the possibilities of a common memory in the Christian community, and it does not bear the possibilities alone, but it is surely the critical document for church's remembering.[41]

For Verhey, to remember means "to own a past as our own past in the continuing church, and to own it as constitutive of identity and determinative for discernment."[42] It often involves storytelling that has the shape of obedience. For example, in remembrance of the story of manna, we are asked not to accumulate riches/lands but to leave some for the poor (Lev 19:9–10). When John Burgess raises a challenge, insisting that Scripture is something more than story—it is a sacramental word and poetry that engages imagination and invites one to construe the world—and that the risen Christ is not just remembered by the Church, Verhey responds arguing that remembering is "itself more than recollection...[and] the real presence of Christ is mediated by our remembering Jesus, by attending to the story."[43]

Specifically, Jesus of Nazareth, who reveals God's good nature to us and sanctifies us, is for Verhey, the center of the Gospel, and his resurrection is the key to Scripture. The memory of Jesus is thus "central to what the Church understands when it understands Scripture."[44] Reading the stories of Jesus is the starting point for using Scripture in ethics. Other stories of the New Testament are only parts of the whole story the evangelists tell in memory of Jesus.[45] Consequently, remembering Jesus is crucial to Christian ethics. This whole hermeneutic of remembering Jesus is best demonstrated in his *Remembering Jesus: Christian Community, Scripture, and the Moral Life*, as well as two subsequent essays on hospitality and healing.[46]

In the first part of this work, Verhey further develops his hermeneutical framework by highlighting the relationship among Christian community, Scripture, and the moral life. He begins with clarifying the tradition and vocation of early Church communities found in the New Testament: they are communities of moral discourse, deliberation, and discernment by being communities of memory. In remembrance, the early Church preserves its identity and sustains a common life worthy of the Gospel. Our contemporary faith community is one that continues this tradition and vocation by remembering the early Church remembering Jesus. Based on specific texts found in certain New Testament writings—such as the narrative of the empty tomb in Luke (24:6–8), the farewell discourse in John (14:26), and later epistles (e.g., 2 Tim 2:8)—Verhey is convinced that the preservation and forming of a Christian community relies on remembering Jesus. Actually, Verhey perceives each Gospel as "a remembrance, a literary commemoration of the crucified and risen Lord, forming character and shaping conduct into something worthy of the gospel."[47] In order to remember him, Christians must read and understand the Bible in which the memory of Jesus is found.

However, as he did elsewhere, Verhey points out the problems encountered when turning to Scripture for moral instruction; hence, he insists that our remembrance "must also entail a reflection on the interpretation of Jesus' teaching…in the counsel of the Church community today" and the use of Scripture must be tested and qualified by a communal discernment.[48]

As a whole, this important section provides a unique perspective for the rest of his discussion. The remaining parts are subsequent applications of the hermeneutics of remembering in various moral contexts—sickness, sexuality, economy, and politics. Each of them is explored "by way of reminder" and follows a similar pattern:[49] (1) The contemporary situation is defined and reflected on. (2) The life and teachings of Jesus regarding the topic is "remembered." (3) The teaching of the early Church remembering Jesus is "remembered." (4) The insights emerging "by way of reminder" are applied to the corresponding ethical issue faced by the Christian community today.

With regards to the scriptural texts used throughout this work, Verhey basically uses the Bible broadly and frequently, though with preference given to the New Testament writings.[50] He usually begins with Old Testament texts to highlight the contemporary issue/situation, then moves on to the teachings of Jesus, and finally that of the early Church communities (related to Paul and other writers) that remember Jesus.[51]

As a whole, Verhey's approach is one that "engages with biblical scholarship, the tradition of the Church and the realities of contemporary life."[52] The study is substantial and informative, and goes beyond the kind of descriptive, chronological approach found in other New Testament ethics writings. The scriptural texts employed are plentiful and appropriate. However, some reviewers rightly note that certain important exegetical studies are either missing or simplified (e.g., the Pauline imperative and indicative). And he seems to fail to attend to certain methodological questions, such as how to determine what the historical Jesus thought and did, and how to identify the normative values of Jesus' life and teachings.

Despite these drawbacks, Verhey builds his work upon a hermeneutic of remembering and a sound ethical model that focuses on practices, community, character development, and narrative. While he is interested in employing scriptural texts in his discussions, he does not forget the importance of ethical hermeneutics. In each of the discussions, he engages in descriptive, synthetic, hermeneutic, and pragmatic tasks. *Remembering Jesus*, as Spohn thus comments, complements Hays's work in the sense that it integrates Hays's four interrelated tasks into a whole.

Last but not least, one reviewer further commends that

Verhey's work "represents the best of a biblical theologian and Christian ethicist at work."[53]

So far, we note how a biblical scholar and a Christian ethicist have made further contributions through their works. Burridge, who comes from the discipline of biblical scholarship, does so by proposing a biographical reading of the scriptural texts. A significant advantage of this approach is that it serves, not just as a tool of exegetical (literary) criticism, but also a sound hermeneutical lens for ethical analysis—one that attends to character, narrative, and practices. Burridge has demonstrated that a more integrated Scripture-based ethics, from the perspective of biblical scholarship, is possible and can be achieved by employing a sound ethical framework for hermeneutics.

Verhey advances from a different direction. He attempts textual interpretation of the Bible just as his biblical counterparts do. His efforts have demonstrated his awareness of the importance of the text in doing biblical ethics. Verhey has thus shown us that a more integrated Scripture-based ethics, from the perspective of theological ethics, is possible and can be achieved by first taking the scriptural text seriously and interpreting the text carefully.

In conclusion, the lengthy survey of current attempts by both disciplines at constructing a more integrated Scripture-based Christian ethics has revealed to us that such a methodological goal is attainable, and concrete advancements are found within each discipline. Specifically, recent works by a biblical scholar and a Christian ethicist have paved the way to part of the position that I advance in this book: doing biblical ethics demands, at the same time, both careful exegesis and interpretation, using a sound ethical framework.

However, this survey also reveals an emerging twofold consensus among these scholars. First, there is the view that the task of exegesis and the task of interpretation are almost *inseparable* in the area of Scripture and ethics. Second, there is the growing *collaboration* between biblical scholars and theological ethicists in doing Scripture-based ethics, especially in terms of writing and teaching. From the perspective of Christian ethics, unfortunately, no consensus is reached on what particular ethical framework should be used as the hermeneutical tool in doing Scripture-based ethics.

Scripture as "Scripted Script"

Whatever biblical theologians may have achieved in offering ethical interpretation for contemporary readers or Christian ethicists in seeking textual interpretation of the original meaning of the text, a genuine Scripture-based ethics would not be possible if one sought to perform one task without the other.

I find a particularly helpful approach in portraying and understanding the inseparability of the exegetical and hermeneutical tasks in Verhey's construal of Scripture as "scripted script."[54] To appreciate the argument, we begin by inspecting the meanings of the two terms, namely, "scripted" and "script." The text as "scripted" means that it was written at a particular time by certain authors. The text as "script" can be grasped by thinking of the script of a play that is acted out by the performer. The performance of any script is itself an interpretation of the script.

Verhey further explores the distinction between "scripted" and "script" by employing the distinction between object and instrument.[55] As "scripted," the written text is "an object to us, a given, the product of the activity of others."[56] It needs to be examined textually in order to know what sort of writing it is. As "script," the text is, in contrast, an instrument for and a vocation (or an invitation) to activity for the reader. These two aspects cannot be separated for the written text is "both the effect of the action of writing texts and the instrument that we use to perform certain other actions."[57]

Verhey invokes the notion of "scripted script" in the context of scriptural ethics in order to understand the different tasks of biblical scholarship and Christian ethics, and to give prominence to the relationship between them. As "scripted," the Bible is studied by those exegetes within the Church community who "bring their knowledge of Hebrew and Greek, or their training in the tools of historical, literary, or social investigation, not just to the texts but to the community."[58] As "script," the Bible is to be performed recurrently "in the rhetoric and practices of the churches, in their theology and in their worship, in their ethics and in their politics."[59] Thus, Christian ethicists looking to the Bible for moral guidance must look to the scriptural texts for the "prompting" toward appropriate actions, practices, and virtues. Even though the task of exegesis is conventionally assigned to biblical scholarship while that of interpretation is given to theological ethicists, Verhey points out that they are so related for it is the Church community that canonized Scripture that interprets and performs Scripture.

As a whole, Verhey developed these notions because of his conviction that the community of faith could not adequately understand the moral guidance of Scripture without studying the text as "scripted" and using it as "script." This conviction points to the need to see Scripture as *both* "scripted" and "script." In other words, the two assigned tasks are actually mutually related and inseparable, and required for whosoever engages in a Scripture-based ethics. He writes, "Attention to Scripture as scripted finally *requires* attention to Scripture as a text appropriately read when it is...performed. And attention to Scripture as script to be performed is surely *enriched* by attention to Scripture as scripted."[60]

When interpreting the text, the interpreter has a responsibility "to make judgments about the sort of text it is, about the whole of which it is a part...about the interest appropriate to it, and about the appropriate use of this object as instrument, the performance of this text."[61] These judgments affect how the text is read and used. However, this is not a purely personal responsibility, for it is the community that owns the Bible as canon: one's reading of the scriptural text is conditioned by (and, therefore, answerable to) the community to which one belongs. The community "exercises interpretative discernment by asking how each part of Scripture as scripted fits the whole."[62]

Similarly, the performance of the script by theological ethicists can be enriched when one carefully attends to what the biblical authors did with the texts at their disposal: different performances may emerge, and, yet, none of them can capture the true meaning of the text/script definitively. Attending to the text can, therefore, function as a test for and guide to performance.

As far as the enterprise of methodological enquiry is concerned, Verhey's emphasis on Scripture as both "scripted" and "script" implies the necessity of engaging in both tasks, and the need to pay equal attention to the importance of the scriptural text and of the ethical hermeneutics in doing biblical ethics. This implication points us in the right direction of doing Scripture-based ethics, and his effort has offered us an apt model of what an integrated Scripture-based ethics can be.

Concrete Collaboration

The emerging consensus among scholars regarding the inseparability of the exegetical and hermeneutical tasks does not simply obtain on the theoretical level but on the practical level as well, especially through concrete collaboration. In fact, signs of collaboration can be traced back to before the 1980s. Some scholars have taken a step further to work hand in hand with colleagues of the other field. One of the earlier joint efforts is the coauthored work of biblical scholar Bruce C. Birch and Christian ethicist Larry L. Rasmussen, entitled *Bible and Ethics in Christian Life*. In this 1976 work, they attempt to "bridge the gap between biblical studies and Christian ethics" and to "address the relationship of Scripture and ethics."[63] Birch and Rasmussen point out that both Christian ethics and biblical scholarship "are called upon most directly to aid the faith community in traversing the distance between the primal documents of the faith—its Scriptures—and expressions of the faith in daily life."[64] Although their pioneer work is primarily a book about moral life and it is only in the last two chapters (excluding the concluding chapter) that they discuss the role of the Bible in moral life, what is most valuable is their methodological proposal that encourages interdisciplinary work. Regrettably, we have not seen much written collaboration since then. Rather, collaboration reemerged in the classroom setting.

Beginning in the 1980s, ethicist William Spohn team-taught with New Testament scholar John Donahue: together they offered courses on New Testament Ethics when they were both faculty members of the then Jesuit School of Theology at Berkeley.[65] For instance, in "The New Testament and Christian Ethics" course, they began with a canonical description of New Testament ethics, including "Jesus' Eschatological Ethics," "The Ethics of the Gospels," "The Christological Ethics of Paul," and "Letter to the Hebrews and the Book of Revelation." Then, they turned to various modes of interpretation, such as liberation, feminist, and narrative hermeneutics, in the second half of the course. However, they did not demonstrate how biblical scholarship and ethical reflection interact in concrete situations.[66]

A more recent and more developed attempt was the work of Daniel Harrington and James Keenan, both from Boston College. Their approach was very different from that of Donahue and Spohn. They have been trying to build a bridge between the two fields through their joint writings and team teaching in the past decade. The motivation behind their collaboration is the fact that both Harrington and Keenan are interested in listening to what the other says and try to accommodate what is heard into their own agenda and reflection. In their coauthored book, *Jesus and Virtue Ethics*, based on their team-taught course bearing the same name, Harrington and Keenan start off a common framework that is built upon certain ethical themes: for example, when discussing the theme of "love as the primary virtue," Harrington first offers an exposition on the love of God and neighbor in Matthew 22:34–40; Keenan then reflects on the primacy of charity proposed by Gerard Gilleman.[67]

At the time of this writing, they team-taught "Paul and Virtue Ethics" several times and published a book with the same title. Here, they likewise interpret the selected moral/ethical teachings of Paul and the Pauline writings through the lens of virtue and engage in interaction between the two tasks. The specific topics covered include, "the shape of Paul's virtue ethics…faith, love, hope, virtues and vices, ethics in a communal setting, social ethics...and sexual morality."[68] They are convinced that "the concerns of Christian virtue ethics provide a good lens for reading Paul's letters, and that Paul and his letters provide a good lens for understanding Christian virtue ethics."[69] In the near future, they are planning to offer a course on "John and Virtue Ethics" and publish another book. These team-taught and joint writing projects illuminate their commitment to bridging the gap and better integrating Scripture and Christian ethics.

Finally, their Jesuit colleagues in the former Weston Jesuit School of Theology in Cambridge, Massachusetts, Hebrew Scripture scholar Richard Clifford and Social ethicist Thomas Massaro also twice team-taught in recent years a course on the Bible and social justice. This seminar course offers students "the opportunity to learn to interpret the social message of the Bible in a way that illustrates contemporary issues of social justice."[70] It explores key elements of contemporary social ethics, such as the meanings of justice, power and authority, the status of women, and environmental responsibility, and examines how the Bible illuminates them. They also introduce certain appropriate ways to use the Bible in ethical reasoning and discourse. Therefore, the course mainly focuses on the use of Scripture in a specific area of ethics. Unfortunately, the use of scriptural texts is rather limited and scattered. And in spite of frequent reference to selective Church documents on Catholic social teaching, there is no particular ethical framework employed.

We see that this theoretical consensus has been put into practice by some scholars through their team teaching and joint publications. In particular, I find that the collaboration of Harrington and Keenan stands out among other examples, especially in terms of their use of a coherent and sound ethical framework.

In the fourth and final chapter, I propose the use of a particular hermeneutics. I take virtue ethics as an apt hermeneutical tool for a variety of reasons.[71] It is argued that a virtue ethics "provides a lens through which to examine the moral life in a richer way than approaches that concentrate solely on actions, rules, and contentious cases."[72]

Within the context of biblical ethics, both Harrington and Keenan point out that virtue ethics is "true to both the New Testament emphasis on the human response to God's gracious activity in Jesus Christ and to the ethical needs and desires of Christians."[73] In addition, as will be discussed later, the various dimensions of virtue have certain advantages over other act- or principle-based ethics in approaching biblical texts. Thus, virtue ethics can be a promising starting point for engaging in deeper conversation between biblical scholars and moral theologians.

Furthermore, among the above-surveyed scholars who have attempted to build upon an ethical framework, not a few turn to virtues and practices for insights on hermeneutics. Burridge, for example, points out that the depiction of character is often implied within a biographical narrative. Although ethical instruction may not be the primary concern of ancient biography, the idea of imitation in which one observes, follows, and practices the subject's virtues is common to much such literature. The case of Verhey, on the other hand, is rather self-evident. Apart from advocating certain virtues for Christian moral life, such as hospitality and justice, he perceives the notion of practice as a core element of Christian ethical framework.

CHAPTER FOUR

A HERMENEUTICAL PROPOSAL

A Hermeneutic of Virtue Ethics

The ethics of virtue is one of the oldest moral philosophies. It has gone through cycles of development, decline, and revival in the past two millennia.[1] Within the western world, for example, Plato was the first to utilize virtues in order to identify the highest good that an individual (and the state) can attain. He also enunciated the classical list of cardinal virtues. However, it was Aristotle who gave us the classic formulation of virtue:[2] it is a disposition that makes a person good and causes the person to perform her/his function well. All virtues are directed toward an end or *telos*—happiness in this life. Since one performs her/his function well only when the mean is observed, Aristotle developed the doctrine of the mean that seeks equidistance between deficiency and excess. He further placed virtue in the genus of habit—it is an irreversible and almost unchangeable condition, and becomes one's second nature over the course of time. Finally, early Greek philosophical reflections on virtues are concerned about not just the good of the individual but of the society as well.

During the patristic period, both Western and Eastern Church Fathers offered their understandings of virtues and highlighted God as the ultimate *telos* for humanity: for Augustine, charity is the ordering virtue for Christian life, and all true virtues are basically different forms of charity. John Chrysostom and John Climacus (of the sixth century) further perceived the acquisition of virtue as central and fundamental to the believer's life.

Medieval scholastic Thomas Aquinas presented to us a systematic classification of virtues in the *Summa Theologiae* (*ST*) (I.II. 55–70):[3] intellectual and moral virtues, theological and cardinal/natural virtues, and infused and acquired virtues. Intellectual and moral virtues perfect the speculative intellect and the appetitive powers, respectively. Theological virtues have God as their object while the cardinal virtues are directed to certain human goods as grasped by reason. However, Aquinas's infused virtues do not only include the theological virtues but also infused cardinal virtues as well. The infused cardinal virtues differ from the acquired cardinal virtues because the former are given by God, aim at the attainment of supernatural happiness, and their object is, indirectly but inevitably, God. Most contemporary scholars would agree that Aquinas framed his discussion theologically (rather than philosophically) and that his theory is basically Augustinian with Aristotelian modifications.

Unfortunately, for various reasons, interest in the virtues began to decline in the subsequent centuries, and the discussion of virtues was slowly replaced by principle and rule-oriented ethics. Within the Catholic tradition, for instance, the manualists of the seventeenth century began to treat Aquinas's theological and moral virtues as sources of obligations for moral living. It was not until the second half of the twentieth century that the retrieval of virtue ethics began to emerge from philosophical, theological, and public sectors.[4]

Within the discipline of philosophy, the beginning of the revival can be traced back to the well-known article of Elizabeth Anscombe ("Modern Moral Philosophy") in 1958. Still, Alasdair MacIntyre's work has been most influential in this retrieval. In *After Virtue*, MacIntyre argues for a multistage logical development of the concept of virtue: each stage requires a corresponding background account—namely, practice, narrative unity, and tradition—through which the complex conception of virtue can be understood. Subsequently, virtue is referred to as dispositions that not only sustain practices but also concern the unity of one's whole life and relate one's individual life to that of the community.

Theologians, in turn, engaged in the discussion of virtue ethics and various schools emerged based on different traditions and emphases. Among Protestant ethicists, Stanley Hauerwas is known for focusing on the notion of character: character is inseparable from one's self-determination and is the decisive factor behind one's doing and becoming. Hauerwas also argues for the primacy and interrelatedness of community and narrative in any moral tradition: the believing community as a moral community is a community of virtue; and virtues are acquired through involvement in the embodiment of the story in one's own community. Other proponents within Protestantism include Gilbert Meilaender and Joseph Kotva. Kotva is especially known for making a Christian case for virtue ethics. His understanding of Scripture in constructing a Christian account of virtue ethics is equally noteworthy. I will return to him in our discussion of relating Scripture with virtue.

The Catholic counterparts are represented by William Spohn, James Keenan, and Jean Porter. Both Keenan and Porter follow the Thomistic approach to virtue, although their views differ from one another. Porter claims that Aquinas's approach to virtue theory is not one of dichotomy—that is, a theory of virtue vis-à-vis a theory of rules—but one that takes up the moralities of both rules and virtues. Keenan, in contrast, sees virtue ethics as a comprehensive system in that, in the pursuit of virtues, we generate norms. He argues that "a virtue based ethics that generates its own norms and principles is more capable of guiding us in action than a simple normative ethics."[5] Along this line, he further argues that all normative ethics inevitably find their origins in a virtue ethics. Moreover, Keenan engages virtue ethics with other areas of morality and proposes a contemporary list of cardinal virtues for ordinary life. And, with Spohn, he also tries to bridge moral theology and other theological disciplines (e.g., spirituality and Scripture) through virtue ethics.

The return to virtue theory is, however, not without challenges and criticisms.[6] For example, some philosophers note that virtue theory's conceptual commitment to the moral agent leads to several shortcomings, especially regarding the place of actions. They are concerned that virtue ethics is structurally incapable of saying much about what one ought to do and, hence, is impractical and inadequate for our complex society. They also charge that such commitment to, and over-focusing on, the agent could lead to self-centeredness. Moreover, there is the challenge of identifying the virtuous person, as well as a kind of over-optimism within virtue theory regarding changing complex society. Theologians further complain that virtue ethics encourages a false sense of one's own good and self-reliance rather than on God's grace, obedience, and self-sacrifice. Those who seek a middle way thus claim that virtue theory is not a complete alternative to moral principles; rather, both are needed should ethics be practical. Despite these criticisms, reflections on the role of virtue ethics continue to flourish within contemporary Christianity.[7]

We need to be mindful that the revival of virtue ethics has produced a bewildering variety of claims made in the name of virtue by contemporary philosophers and theologians, such as consequential and non-consequential virtue ethics.[8] In the case of Christian virtue ethics, Porter similarly reminds us that we cannot simply assume that the Aristotelian or Thomistic tradition is the only option either. She writes, "[T]heologians today are turning to virtue ethics out of a variety of different concerns. For this reason, it would be a mistake to assume that there is one definitive form of virtue ethics, or even that all virtue ethicists would agree about the meaning and implications of the concept of virtue."[9]

In the following pages, I look at the contemporary understanding of virtue theory in a particular way that is fitting to our schema. First, I identify five common characteristics of virtue ethics. Second, I introduce four important dimensions of virtue ethics that emerge from these characteristics. Third, three related issues regarding the implication and adaptation of virtue theory in our discussion of biblical ethics are presented. Fourth, I explore how two Christian virtue ethicists relate Scripture and virtue, and, from there, I present my own approach of relating Scripture and virtue ethics, an approach grounded in those four dimensions of virtue.

Common Characteristics of Virtue Ethics

Grounded in the above-mentioned historical development, there are certain essential features shared by many proponents of virtue ethics (although different proponents have different emphases). I identify five common characteristics that allow us to acquire a contemporary understanding of virtue ethics. First, virtue ethics is a teleological ethics. In general, the ethics of virtue that is based on Aristotelian and Thomistic understanding of virtue is "an ethic premised on the notion of a true human nature with a determinate human good or end or *telos*."[10] This *telos*, or good, is originally defined as performing well whatever is characteristic of the subject, such as its function, purpose, or role, and upon which its evaluation lies. When applied to human persons, it implies that who we are and what we do can be evaluated "against our true nature or *telos*, against the excellent performance of the functions and purposes characteristic of human."[11] Aristotle, for example, famously proposed that the ultimate human end is *eudaimonia* (happiness) in this life.

However, in the case of human *telos*, one needs to know the sort of capacities, traits, and interests the person has that allows one to pursue the good.[12] Also, the human *telos* is not a narrowly defined or restrictive one but rather a comprehensive and inclusive one. While specific *teloi* are needed for the provision of guidance for acquiring virtues, this does not mean that one is guided by certain narrow visions of the human good only.

Second, virtue ethics has a particular, dynamic structure. An ethical theory as such is concerned with not just who we are but also who we could become, and is thus a teleological ethics with a particular structure. Keenan refines MacIntyre's tri-polar structure of virtue ethics into three fundamental questions.

First is the question of who one is—"Who am I?" In the language of virtue ethics, this question is equivalent to asking oneself how virtuous one is. The answer to this question lies in the standards of measurement and the fairness of such measurement. The former refers to the naming of the basic virtues while the latter implies critical self-knowledge of one's spontaneous actions.

The second question asks, "Who ought I become?" It points to our vision and, hence, invites us to set our personal goals and articulate our *teloi* by means of speculative reason. The key insight here is that one has to pursue them and seek improvement.

The third and last question asks what actions will move one from the present self to one's future self—"What ought I to do?" It focuses on both the tension between "who we are" and "who we could be," and how we move from the former state to the latter. It points to those transformative virtuous acts (i.e., practices), and their effectiveness depends on the virtue of prudence through which one not just articulates one's realistic ends but also sets to attain them.

Furthermore, based on the important presupposition that the kind of person one will become tomorrow is shaped by one's action today, it is argued that virtue ethics is historically dependent and has a dynamic structure. The real world in which one lives is a necessity for the tri-polar structure because without it virtue ethics could become narcissistic.

Third, virtue ethics is concerned about human good. Although different ethicists propose different understandings of the qualities of the human *telos,* they generally agree that it is largely constituted by the exercise and practice of various virtues. However, virtues are not simply means or instruments to, but also constituted elements and essential components of, the human good. This twofold view of virtue can be understood as follows. A virtue is "an acquired human quality the possession of which tends to enable us to achieve those goods which are internal to practices and the lack of which effectively prevents us from achieving any such goods."[13] It is thus an instrument and means to the human good. Yet, Spohn rightly claims that it is also a constitutive element of the human *telos,* because the values one seeks would characterize the way that one pursues them. Virtues, then, are human goods in themselves. We act hospitably, for instance, because it leads to the human good and is virtuous itself.

Fourth, virtue theorists are interested in moral character and, thus, give priority to being over doing. Virtues are acquired dispositions that include both "tendencies to react in characteristic ways in similar and related settings…[and] all those states of character or character traits that influence how we act and choose."[14] This understanding is drawn upon Aristotle's view that virtues are character traits that are needed to live flourishing lives. For example, virtues, such as benevolence and justice, feature among those intrinsic goods without which one cannot have a flourishing life. Subsequently, virtues are states of character that have long ranging impact in us.

Apart from giving primacy to character, virtue theory actually attends to the development of character and the practices of the person and the community. As seen in its tri-polar structure, virtue ethics is concerned with "who we ought to become." However, it is important to remember that virtue ethics, like any ethics, recommends action, but first recommends the kind of persons we should become and, then, informs the choices and actions. As we have seen, Aristotle taught that virtue makes persons good and causes them to act well. In this sense, virtue ethics gives priority of being over doing. Still, we become a more virtuous person only by performing intended virtuous actions. In other words, one's being is formed in and through "doing," and while "being" paves the way for "doing," "doing" shapes "being."

Fifth, the ethics of virtue bears a kind of perfectionism. Such perfectionism has to be understood in the sense of "viewing all aspects of life as morally relevant and in calling everyone to growth in every area of life."[15] Virtue ethics, as such, is seen as a proactive ethical system that encompasses one's entire life, for each knowingly performed moral action affects the kind of moral person one becomes. It engages the commonplace and concerns what is ordinary rather than those exceptional moral dilemmas. In addition, since virtues are teleological by nature, they are heuristic and collectively aim for the right realization of human identity.

The Four Dimensions of Virtue Ethics

Besides acquiring a contemporary understanding of virtue theory, we need to ask ourselves if the virtues help us to appreciate better the fullness of the moral life? For instance, do the virtues help us to look beyond the self to the community and other people? I say yes precisely because virtue ethics has extensive dimensions to its overall thesis. I, hereby, introduce four of them: (1) dispositions and character formation; (2) practices and habits; (3) exemplar; and (4) community and communal identity. They not only help us understand better the moral life but also make virtue a fuller ethical framework by serving as reference points to the task of hermeneutics.

Dispositions and Character Formation

Some proponents of virtue ethics would define the ethics of virtue as "ethics of character." They claim that character ethics "does not altogether neglect rules, but subordinates them to the development of moral character and views them instrumentally with reference to the end."[16] It refers to "a way of thinking about and interpreting the moral life in terms of a particular vision of and a passion for life that is rooted in the nurture, formation, and socialization of a particular self-conscious community."[17]

Hauerwas, in particular, rediscovers virtues through his ethics of character. He sees character as inseparable from one's self-determination and as the decisive factor behind our doing and becoming. Hauerwas further asserts that "character is not just the sum of all that we do as agents, but rather it is the particular direction our agency acquires by choosing to act in some ways rather than others."[18] Interestingly, this emphasis on character can be found in Burridge's own thinking: he points out that the depiction of character is often implied within a biographical narrative. In the case of the New Testament, the Gospels, as biographical narrative, aim to characterize Jesus by looking at his authority, integrity, and service of others.

Nevertheless, I claim that character formation is an important dimension of virtue. In classical virtue theory, the question of the good life leads directly to the development of moral character, because "any adequate description of a good human life will necessarily include attributes that are not manifest in persons in the beginning of their lives, but are developmental outcomes."[19]

Virtues are "excellences of character that are objective goods, of worth to others [and the self]," and their manifestation is the actualization of qualities that are originally potentialities within a person.[20] Moreover, since virtue ethics is concerned about "who we could become" and the transition from "who we are" to "who we could become" (i.e., the movement toward the human *telos*), it calls for continual growth in our character.

In addition, the acquisition and development of virtue demands our understanding of the self as a self-forming and determining agent who shapes her or his own: our choices and actions help form our tendencies and dispositions, which, in turn, help inform and direct our subsequent choices and actions. One thus plays a role in the formation of one's character. For example, the practice of hospitality makes us hospitable persons, which, in turn, directs us to act hospitably. What is central to the development of moral character is the achievement of integrity—by which all the dimensions of a person, such as faculties, desires, dispositions, and roles, contribute to the chosen end. In this fashion, the ethics of virtue is all about moral formation.

On the other hand, since a person's character is "the integration of [one's] life into a relatively coherent unity" and the identity of a person is formed when this integrated self is conscious, virtue ethics thus, as Spohn claims, inevitably considers identity.[21] In line with Spohn's view, Keenan further notes that there is interplay between virtues and an anthropological vision of human identity: virtues provide practical guides to the right realization of identity while the anthropological vision of human identity guides us in our pursuit of the virtues.

Practices and Habits

The ethics of virtue is more interested in the ordinary than in neuralgic moral dilemmas or extremely grave actions. It is concerned about what one ought to do in daily life as one moves from "who I am" to "what I ought to become." These concerns can best be handled by developing practices. Regarding practice, MacIntyre writes,

> By a "practice" I am going to mean any coherent and complex form of socially established cooperative human activity through which goods internal to that form of activity are realized in the course of trying to achieve those standards of excellence which are appropriate to, and partially definitive of, that form of activity, with the result that human powers to achieve excellence, and human conceptions of the ends and goods involved, are systematically extended.[22]

Simply put, practice is a regular activity that forms us in such a way that certain dispositions to act in particular ways are developed. For MacIntyre, virtue belongs to the concept of practice.

When we continuously adopt practices in our ordinary life, we form habits. Habits, in turn, "become deeply ingrained in and constitute particular dimensions of our lives…and make us who we are."[23] Aristotle understands habit as a kind of irremediable condition that is like a "second nature" for the individual. Aquinas adopts this basic view and further perceives habits as qualities or principles of action that employ the will and are in relation to the definition of virtue (*ST* I.II. 49.1–3). In this fashion, he seems to understand virtue as a habit (*ST* I.II. 55.4). Spohn, however, argues that by treating virtues as practices rather than as habit, one is able to "appreciate the social formation of the virtues and enable [one] to consider the regulative internal norms [such as motive, roles, and other virtues] of the virtues."[24]

Nevertheless, we acquire virtues by habitually acting virtuously. For instance, if we want to become hospitable as a person and as a community, we have to act hospitably. At some point, we so condition ourselves to this way of acting that we become hospitable. Once we acquire hospitality, then, like a second nature, we act hospitably easily and almost naturally whenever we meet someone new. In this way, we will be more ready to welcome the stranger than if we have not practiced hospitality.

The above interpretation, in one way or another, helps us understand Verhey's emphasis on the notion of practice as a core element of Christian ethical framework, and that remembering

Jesus requires participation in the practices of the Church community. Indeed, practices both develop the characters of the moral agent and, in turn, express them. It points us back to the previous dimension of virtue—the formation of character.

Exemplar[25]

Besides attending to character, virtue theory also appreciates the role exemplary figures play in the development of virtue and formation of character. This appreciation is grounded in the fundamental presupposition that virtue is teachable.[26] Historically, according to Meilaender, Plato made it clear that examples of moral virtue are transmitted only through storytelling that provides an "inborn affinity" for the knowledge of the good. However, Plato also suggested that the teaching of virtue can be achieved by "the study not of ethics but of other disciplines."[27]

Burridge also points out that, although ethical instruction may not be the primary concern of ancient biography, the idea of imitation, in which one imitates, follows, and practices the good example's virtues, is common to such literature. Within Christianity, Eastern Church Father Athanasius claimed that "the practice of imitating the exemplars of the faith is fundamental to the acquisition of Christian virtue…[and] transformation by way of the imitation of the mentor's life of virtue may result in communion, in a sharing of vision."[28] Climacus was further convinced that a guide or a mentor, who has struggled on the ladder of virtue, would have the vision and critical discernment needed for guiding others. These claims and convictions affirm that the idea of imitation and the need and role of a mentor are closely related.

Mentors, guides, and exemplars are needed in two ways. First, the virtues as skills need examples to show what they mean practically. Second, they teach and encourage us to act likewise. Spohn explains that virtues "have to be displayed concretely to convey their tactical meaning. In order to grasp, [for example], how courage and integrity operate, we need accounts of persons who have shown these virtues in the tangle of circumstances. We are more likely to learn these lessons from literature than philosophy."[29] For instance, in the Hebrew Bible, Judith has been viewed as a model for liberation and the embodiment of the virtue of courage; Ruth and Naomi also illustrate the values of loyalty and love of family.

In our contemporary society, Andrew Flescher points out that there are two notable types of exemplar. The first type is heroes, such as rescuers. Heroes are "not mere moral paragons but exemplars, demonstrations of human beings living the best kind of moral life."[30] Though they distinguish themselves by excelling, heroes are ordinary persons, represent and act (already) the way we should; the life they live is "in principle accessible to anyone who becomes sufficiently virtuous."[31] Nevertheless, they are extraordinarily virtuous and we need to act as they do.

The second type, saints, differs from heroes in many ways. Specifically, they "transcend their 'exemplar' status and come to embody a higher law."[32] Saints are thus distinctive moral agents who are extraordinarily virtuous, visionary, and embody "an ideal of character that is not fully realizable by ordinary agents in the course of a life."[33] They have no limits regarding what is morally required of them. Some further perceive saints as acquiring all the moral virtues to an extreme degree.

The differences between heroes and saints further highlight the two different senses of "exemplar": the example of heroes "instantiates and thus clarifies general principles of morality and qualities of character that can be articulated as meaningful and understood as possible for all participants in a society or community."[34] The morality of saints is, in contrast, above ordinary morality and, hence, it is exemplary in the sense that it "motivates us from afar, as a future ideal that impinges on us in the present."[35]

Although moral saints are extraordinary persons, one could still aspire to sainthood in general. We should also remember that, like heroes, particular saints exemplify "only certain types of sainthood, and [those] other types may be compatible with quite different human excellences."[36]

In sum, exemplary models inspire and instruct us to be virtuous. Both heroes and saints are much needed in our society. They give us not just concrete guidance in the process of formation but, at times, "challenge us toward the *telos*, and toward fuller embodiment of the virtues."[37] Because of the specificity of their heroism or saintliness, they further reawaken us to appreciating a neglected virtue or a forgotten way of being.

Community and Communal Identity

Virtue ethics has often been criticized as self-centered and virtues as simply subjective dispositions. However, there are important arguments for a communal aspect within virtue theory. The first group of arguments focuses on the roles of community in relation to virtues. First, other than mentors and exemplars, narratives and community facilitate the practice of virtue. Second, community plays an important role in the understanding of the virtues. Thus, the same virtue can be expressed differently in different places. For example, hospitality in a Confucian society like Korea may differ from hospitality in the United States of America. Third, the community, being a historical place that has a tradition, is the proper locus in which the people can understand themselves, recognize the appropriate *telos* of the community, and articulate the virtues they need to develop. Fourth, there is interplay between virtues and an anthropological vision of human identity. Virtue ethics considers identity as not just personal but also communal, for our human identity needs a story, a temporal framework that "synthesizes our diverse moments of experience into a coherent whole."[38] Personal identity "comes through a process of identification with [this] larger narrative framework—a story—and with a community that tries to live out this story."[39] In other words, certain narratives of community define, set limits, and configure personal identity through the ideals they present to us. Thus, the individual finds her/his moral identity in and through her/his membership in a community. However, the community must be vigilant against becoming "closed," for that will only lead to sectarianism.

The second group of arguments for a communal aspect in virtue theory lies in the nature of virtue itself. MacIntyre claims that virtue is a social quality and always demands the taking of certain features of one's social and moral life for its application. As a quality, virtue is needed for "the pursuit of a good for human beings the conception of which is elaborated and possessed within an ongoing social tradition."[40] Thus, some virtue ethicists would understand the human *telos* as flourishment in both a social and a personal way.

This understanding highlights that the nature of a human good is also corporate. There are two major claims here. First, human good is not conceived singularly in individual terms. Moral education and improvement need the presence of others, such as mentors and role models; we depend on each other for moral development; and the community provides an important resource for the moral growth of each of us. Second, the human *telos* and the journey toward this end are found in shared activities and relationships. For Aristotle, the good of a human being is correspondingly and equally good for those with whom one is bound in human community. A community is "a common project that brings about some good recognized as their shared good by all those engaging the project."[41] The central bond of a community is the shared understanding of, and the shared vision of, goods.

However, many virtues depend on social connections within a community that provide the "form and mode" in which the human good is realized—that is, they give "point and purpose" to these virtues. Aristotle thus insists that virtues also find their place in the life of the *polis* (the city). The virtue of friendship, for example, "arises within a relationship defined in terms of a common allegiance to and a common pursuit of goods."[42] Aquinas's understanding of the virtue of justice is similarly social: general justice has the common good of the community as its object (*ST* II.II. 58.5–6). Keenan likewise points out that the theological virtues and the cardinal virtues have enormous social ramifications—they perfect us in the different forms of social relationships that distinguish us.

The relationship between virtue and community, however, is not one sided. Since the time of Plato and Aristotle, virtues "exist not primarily for private purpose, but to form and improve our communities."[43] Hauerwas even claims that certain virtues are necessary should the faith community intend to sustain its existence. Insofar as our identity depends on the community, our character formation is equally communal. Thus, within the community, we seek not only to become virtuous persons but also a particular kind of community.

By way of conclusion, Verhey's advocacy of practices within the faith community illuminates us regarding the relationship between the community and virtue ethics:

> People facing choices and longing for wisdom and virtue are more likely to find help in such a community than in a book on Christian ethics. Precisely as a practical discipline Christian ethics depends upon such a community, relies upon its "goodness" and "knowledge," and points to it to help people think and talk about their choices. The task of Christian ethics is to serve such communities and their moral discourse and discernment, not to attempt to be a substitute for them.[44]

Issues Concerning Cultural and Theological Adaptation

The insights on community as an important dimension of virtue lead to three related questions that are prerequisite to our exploration of relating Scripture and virtue ethics. First, there is the question of cultural contextualization. Specifically, virtue theorists' emphasis on the local community raises the concerns about cultural relativism.[45] Proponents of virtue ethics generally believe that every culture has a set of virtues to guide its people to answer the question of what kind of community they should become. Among them, a few believe that each set of virtues is specific only to that particular culture and, thus, argue for a "thick," local understanding of virtues. Many, however, believe that virtues from different cultures can be analogously compared. In other words, there are trans-cultural similarities between virtues of different cultures. Some further argue that there are universal virtues, or at least "thin" virtues in all cultures. Consequently, we see a spectrum of views, ranging from those who believe in cultural contextualization to those who want to transcend the boundary of local culture. I am inclined to take the more progressive view here: though virtues are context sensitive, they are not ultimately relative to a limited context or culture but remain open to revision in light of new circumstances.[46] And it is centered on this view that the undertaking of bringing a virtue-based reading of Scripture into other cultural and religious systems becomes possible. However, such an undertaking inevitably leads to a second, religious question—the question of theological relevance—that I now treat.

As noted earlier, Aquinas classifies virtues into theological and cardinal virtues. Theological virtues are basically virtues infused by God. Cardinal moral virtues, in contrast, have a certain naturalness about them and can be acquired by both Christians and nonbelievers. Moreover, the kind of inner-worldly virtuous acts done by Christians are sometimes distinguished from those by nonbelievers: the former has the supernatural destiny as its goal and grace as its source.

However, are graced virtues outside the faith community possible? In other words, is it possible to find comparable infused theological virtues in non-Christian communities? Here we face the same issue that is found in the question of cultural contextualization: are infused theological virtues specific only to the Christian community or can they be analogously compared? According to Karl Rahner, graced virtue is possible outside the Church community. Again, I take the progressive view in approaching this issue: while the virtues emerged from Scripture are the result of Christian faith and have God's assistance as their source, they can still be engaged cross-culturally with the non-Christian society. A classic example is the virtue of hope.

The third question deals with translating philosophical language into a theological one. This question is directly related to the issue of employing this moral philosophy as a hermeneutical tool for interpreting Scripture. Kotva suggests several fundamental points of references for bridging moral philosophy and theological ethics.[47] The first is the notion of Christian anthropology. Kotva notes that there are similarities between Christian anthropology and virtue theory's understanding of human agency and communal nature. A virtue framework understands that "being" informs "doing" and, yet, our choices and actions shape our character and play an important role in our character formation. A Christian anthropological perspective, in a similar way, while it understands that human freedom is capable of choosing and intending the kind of person one becomes, would also understand that our freedom is limited as a result of our finiteness and sin, and grace is needed for our liberation. Christian anthropology would also affirm the importance of relationships and fellowships with (and service to) God and others. This affirmation is in tune with virtue theory's interest in and emphasis on community and communal identity.

Second, sanctification, like virtuous character formation itself, is a teleological process. But in the theological enterprise, the Christian *telos* is one's conformity with Christ. Its beginning, continuation, and completion radically depend on God's grace (which does not negate one's participation and responsibility for growth). Thus, within a theological setting, the concept of virtue is tied to the notion of grace. Moreover, the *telos* as an ideal and perfection is, in both settings, a goal beyond this world.

The third point of reference is Christology. Theological ethics perceives Jesus Christ as the *telos*. He is the paradigmatic person whose humanity realizes our full human potential and offers us the content of our human *telos*. Jesus is the norm of humanity; and a virtue framework affirms Jesus as normative humanity. Finally, Jesus' call to discipleship finds similarities with the above discussed dimension of virtue (in other contexts), especially in the need and role of exemplary figures.

Both the questions of religious relevance and of translating philosophical language into theological language further point to the relationship between virtue and grace. We understand that moral goodness conveys the agent as striving to realize right living; still, the degree of striving in one's life depends not on oneself but the gifts one receives. From a Christian point of view, it points to the gifts God gives each of us. Within the Catholic tradition, the impact of the gifts of the Holy Spirit has been highlighted even if the Spirit was not directly mentioned.[48]

While theological ethicists rightly retrieved the Christological dimension of ethics, a pneumatological dimension of ethics is also needed; for the Holy Spirit has always been our primary resource for moral life. And although the focus upon the third person of the Trinity has developed slowly, many would agree that the commonly employed language of grace is simply a shorthand for speaking of the Spirit acting.

Aquinas has offered a systematic view of how the Holy Spirit, virtues, and grace are related in the *Summa Theologiae*. He begins with a discussion of the seven gifts of the Holy Spirit, such as understanding, fear, and piety, in light of habit and in relation to virtue (*ST* I.II. 68–70). The gifts of the Holy Spirit have certain characteristics. First, as "gifts" they are infused by God. Second, they are perfections of humankind by which one is disposed and is open to the promptings of God. They are thus related to virtues and are virtues in this particular sense. Third, the gifts of the Holy Spirit are also "habitual dispositions of the soul, rendering it amenable to the motion of the Holy Ghost" (*ST* I.II. 68.3; II.II. 121.1). Fourth, although they are more perfect than the intellectual and moral virtues, they are regulated and preceded by theological virtues. In other words, they seem to link natural virtues with theological virtues and elevate them. Fifth, each theological and cardinal virtue has its own corresponding gifts. For instance, the virtue of faith contains the corresponding gifts of knowledge and understanding (*ST* II.II. 8, 9).

Aquinas later examines the notion of grace and points out that grace as a gift, not only heals our corrupted nature, but also perfects our nature so that we can carry out those meritorious works of supernatural virtue and participate in the divine good (*ST* I.II. 109–114). Hence, grace is supernatural, infused by God, and is teleological. Moreover, grace is gratuitous and produces certain effects: it elevates, justifies, sanctifies, and allows us to be moved by God to act virtuously. It is, therefore, prior to virtues. However, grace differs from infused virtues in that the former is the participation of the divine nature while the latter is derived from and is ordained to this light of grace.

Aquinas further discusses grace as particular gifts of the Holy Spirit (e.g., the gift of tongues) that pertain to certain people for the sake of the community, and are manifested within the communal context (*ST* II.II. 171–78). Grace, as gifts of the Holy Spirit, thus is in line with the fourth important dimension of virtue.

For Aquinas, virtue and grace are closely related and both are gifts of the Holy Spirit. Still, we are also reminded that our dependence on God's grace and the priority of God's grace in our transformation does not mean a passive dependence; rather, God's grace calls for our responsibility and active participation with God in the process of transformation.

Relating Scripture and Virtue Ethics

Virtue, indeed, has a place in theology. Grounded in this affirmation, I now proceed to show how virtue and Scripture are related. I turn to two Christian ethicists for insights because both of them are pioneers in, and well-known advocates of, a Christian virtue ethics within their own traditions. Joseph Kotva lays the ground for making reading Scripture through the lens of virtue possible and desirable. William Spohn further demonstrates a unique, practical way of reading Scripture through the lens of virtue that engages the reader and the biblical texts on the level of ethical practice.

Joseph Kotva, Jr.[49]

Joseph Kotva is an Anabaptist Mennonite. He anchors himself in the neo-Aristotelian (and Thomistic) tradition of virtue and proposes a Christian version of the theoretical ethics of virtue in his *The Christian Case for Virtue Ethics*. Many agree that he has made his case successfully. Throughout this work, Kotva tries to demonstrate that both the Christian doctrines and biblical texts have important "points of similarity, contact and correlation" with virtue theory.[50] What is particularly important to our own enquiry is that he shows, in concrete terms, how Scripture and virtue ethics can be compatible and connected. Kotva argues that, on the one hand, "the *telos* governs the main concerns of biblical theology;" on the other hand, there are biblical convictions about the human good.[51] For instance, Mark 10:13–16 and Luke 14:12–14 can be helpful to grasp a particular aspect of the vision of human good, namely, welcoming the least among us.

Still, Kotva focuses on correlating concretely and specifically the ethics of Matthew and Paul with virtue theory for two reasons: first, they are representatives of the two main genres (namely, Gospels and epistles) in the New Testament. Second, they both seem to be incompatible with virtue ethics at first glance. A successful case with these two texts will make the overall case more convincing. As a whole, Kotva argues that "their concerns, themes, patterns of moral reasoning, and uses of language fit well with the basic virtue framework."[52]

The Gospel of Matthew is usually read as "supporting either a law-based ethics (5:17–18) or an ethic based on the principle of love (22:36–40)."[53] Still, reading the Gospel through the lens of virtue is not just possible but also compatible. First, Matthew is concerned with not just external actions but also the internal qualities of human actions (e.g., feelings and dispositions) as virtue theory is. One significant example is the Beatitudes (5:3–12) that depicts not only the kind of action but also the kind of people that will be received into God's kingdom. These blessings also "commend a posture reflecting certain attitudes and feelings [such as mercy and integrity]."[54] Similarly, some of the antitheses (5:21–48) focus on internal feelings (e.g., anger and lust) rather than external acts. In the parables of good and evil fruits (e.g., 3:8, 10) as well as Jesus' compassionate acts (e.g., 14:14), Matthew likewise "presumes a connection between the internal and the external…[and] one's conduct (the external) flows from and reflects one's inner character (the internal)."[55] Both the connection and priority of the internal over the external are found in virtue theory's near circular relationship between being and doing, and between character states and action.

Second, Matthew manifests a particular kind of perfectionist thrust: the rigorous teaching of the Sermon on the Mount and instruction on discipleship (e.g., 5:48) summon us to have righteousness that exceeds that of the scribes and Pharisees and seek perfection. However, according to Kotva, Matthew is not thinking of a kind of unrealistically idealistic perfection. Rather, Matthew's perfectionism/ideal is to be understood as the norm and guide for discipleship. Moreover, the Gospel writer is aware of the difficulties in achieving the ideal and, therefore, never idealizes the disciples (8:26). It is in this sense that the ethics of Matthew is a perfectionist ethic. However, although Matthew is not expecting a full realization of such an ideal here and now, it does not mean that one needs not to strive for the ideal.

Third, Matthew's portrayal of a master-disciple, instructive relationship between Jesus and his disciples (e.g., 10:24–25) is comparable to the kind of exemplary model suggested by virtue ethics. The only difference is that the relationship between Jesus and his disciples is deeper, more demanding, and more empowering than the relationship between the exemplar and the imitator within the virtue framework.

Fourth, the kind of communal/corporate nature found in virtue theory is also present in the ethics of Matthew. Specifically, Matthew's concerns for community life parallel virtue theory's emphasis that the individual's moral life is found in the communal context and that virtues have a social quality. One significant incidence is the process for Church discipline in chapter 18. Both the wrongdoings ("sins") and their moral discernment are never simply personal matters. They affect the community and are of concern to the community (18:15–17). Furthermore, the underlying qualities of humility and forgiveness (18:4, 21–35) are crucial to the community's unity and maintenance. Here, both Matthean ethics and virtue ethics assume a link between relationships and virtues: the importance of certain virtues is only found in relationships and communal activities. Still, Matthew is equally concerned for concrete individuals (e.g., Jesus' call to specific disciples).

Fifth, Matthew not only portrays Jesus as a master; he also depicts and discusses those character traits through the portrayal of Jesus and various characters in his narratives, such as the centurion in 8:5–13. This mechanism of focusing on character and character traits provides another connection with virtue theory.

Besides showing us that both the moral reasoning and certain qualities of virtue are found in the ethics of Matthew, Kotva also skillfully turns the common view that Matthean ethics is one of law-based or love-centered into another potential link. There are many other types of ethical material in Matthew, such as eschatological warnings and the call to discipleship. The ethics of Matthew is similarly one of mercy (9:13), cross-bearing (10:38), and justice (12:18), and, hence, cannot be adequately or solely summarized by the command to love. The form and content of love is also problematic; for love understood by Matthew has diverse meanings—such as praying for one's enemies (5:44)—and can be known clearly only within particular contexts/narratives. In addition, Matthean ethics is not simply an affirmation/fulfillment of the Mosaic Law; rather, the authority depends on Jesus who is the norm.

While rules and laws play a vital role in the Gospel, they are not a comprehensive set of commands but "exemplar[s]...pointers to the kind of life expected in the community...paradigms...descriptions of behavior suitable to the coming kingdom...[and] specifications of who we are to become."[56] Therefore, the laws have an educative value, in that they are not an end in themselves but "a language that educates us to the ways of Christ, which are centered on the virtues."[57] This view is comparable to virtue theory's perception of rules as "guides in shaping character for those who do not yet possess practical wisdom."[58] Furthermore, both Matthew's ethics and virtue ethics call for discernment in applying rules (because some commands are greater than others [e.g., 22:37–40]). In the language of virtue, this discernment points to the virtue of practical wisdom or prudence.

It is the general understanding that Paul is "preoccupied with grace and faith [and] leaves little room for ethics, let alone an ethic focusing on the formation of virtuous people."[59] Nevertheless, those compatible links between Matthew's ethics and virtue ethics are also present in the ethics of Paul. First, Paul's appropriation of those "virtue and vice" lists (e.g., Gal 5:22–23; Rom 1:29–31) as well as his desire for our inner conversion and transformation (e.g., 2 Cor 7:1; Gal 4:6) reveal his fundamental concerns for internal qualities. Second, although Paul does not portray particular characters in detail as Matthew does, his frequent call to imitate him who imitates Christ (e.g., 1 Cor 4:16, 11:1) or other worthy examples, such as the Macedonians (2 Cor 8:1–15) is equally comparable to virtue theory's demand of exemplary models. Third, like Matthew, Paul also envisions the Christian life in terms of individual and communal identity. Apart from explicit instructions on unity and mutual concern within the community (e.g., 1 Cor 11:17–34), Paul's use of the body image (e.g., 1 Cor 12:12–31) and teachings on excommunication and supporting the weak (e.g., 1 Cor 5:1–8; 1 Thess 5:14) reflect his emphasis on cooperation and interdependence. Still, Paul does not neglect individual efforts and responsibilities—he often reminds the people that they will be judged by God according to their works (Rom 2:6). Fourth, Paul, like Matthew, highlights the need for discernment and practical wisdom. For instance, the communities are challenged to test and discern everything together (e.g., 1 Thess 5:21; 1 Cor 14:29).

Apart from these common links, Kotva remarkably notes two additional, unique aspects of Paul's ethics that are potentially compatible to virtue theory. The first one is Paul's rather frequent employment of images of moral growth and progress, such as "walking" and "transforming" in Romans 6:4 and 2 Corinthians 3:18, respectively. This vision of moral growth, together with the emphasis on continuity and patterns of behavior, can become a connection point with virtue ethics.

The second one is the famous indicative-imperative modes found in Paul's many writings. Their relationship assumes a link between "being" and "doing"—the indicative mode signifies "who we are as Christians" and the imperative mode signifies the kind of actions that follow naturally from what Paul says in the indicative mode. Like virtue theory's priority of "being" over "doing," Paul also seems to assume the priority of what is said in the indicative statement. Moreover, within Paul's eschatological framework, they are comparable to the tri-polar structure of virtue theory—the indicative mode signifies both "who we are" and "who we ought to become" while the imperative mode signifies those habits and actions that respond to the question of how to get there.[60]

In conclusion, both Paul and Matthew are interested in internal qualities, appealing to exemplary models, individual, and corporate. The ethics of particular New Testament writings also have specific areas of concerns and patterns that are similar to that of virtue theory, such as perfection and moral growth. For Kotva, Scripture and virtue ethics further complement and mutually elucidate each other: virtue ethics explores concerns and themes (e.g., the moral role of friendship[61]) that are not fully treated in Scripture and, hence, enrich (and expand) our Christian moral vision. Scripture, in return, helps illustrate the human good and shapes our understanding of particular virtues by means of its narratives. The Bible offers "vital resources for correcting, refining, and developing a virtue framework," such as the centrality of the person of Jesus and the need of grace.[62]

Kotva's groundbreaking attempt to seek links between Scripture and virtue theory, however, is not without technical criticisms, such as his interpretation of virtue and law language in Matthew: critics argue that Kotva seems to fail to show why and how a virtue ethics interpretation of the law language is better than the Kantian one.[63] However, we have to bear in mind that Kotva's work is only an introductory attempt to make a Christian model of virtue ethics sensible to Christians. In fact, Spohn finds Kotva's treatments of these biblical texts particularly insightful in that they "display the advantages of a virtue interpretation and the points where they correct and advance the framework."[64] I now turn to Spohn's own reading of Scripture for additional insights.

William C. Spohn

As we saw in chapter 2, Spohn has shown great interest in engaging Scripture with ethics. Specifically, he proposes the use of virtue theory as the hermeneutical tool for reading Scripture. For instance, in his earlier work *What Are They Saying about Scripture and Ethics?* Spohn claims that the model of "responsive love" best represents his view (in comparison to other approaches) of using and reading Scripture; for this model spells out the implications of virtue ethics, focuses on the moral agent, and guides the agent to respond to the question of "What ought I to do?" Virtue ethics, he adds, is capable of raising "the imaginative and affective dimensions of moral experience to critical reflection to show...how pervasive the guidance of Scripture can be in the mature Christian and the authentic Christian community."[65]

Later, in *Go and Do Likewise: Jesus and Ethics*, Spohn presents three arguments for the appropriateness of virtue ethics in reading Scripture. First and foremost, he turns to the notions of character and narrative. Since virtue ethics attends to one's character while Scripture discloses the character of God, virtue theory is a suitable way to approach Scripture. Moreover, since narrative sets the structure of the Bible while characters are defined over the course of the story, the use of the moral category of character helps us to grasp the ethical import of scriptural texts that relate to a person's life story. In the case of the New Testament, the character of Jesus is revealed through the story of his life.

Second, both virtue ethics and Scripture are concerned about the "heart": biblical writers emphasize the "heart"—"the personal center that infuses acts with meaning"—and "probe the motivations and intentions behind action and the basic orientation of life."[66] In the Sermon on the Mount, for instance, Jesus "seeks a more radical 'righteousness' in the heart [rather than] offer[s] a detailed code of conduct."[67] Virtue theory, likewise, focuses on those inner dynamics of dispositions, habits, and emotions that are the sources of one's personal moral life.

Third, both virtue theory and Scripture (the Gospels, in particular) stress the importance of moral paradigms for guidance. Spohn takes on Hays's view that "paradigms are the most basic vehicle for moral teaching in the New Testament" through which the moral norms are specified.[68] These biblical paradigms exercise, therefore, a normative role in moral reflection. For example, the parable of the Good Samaritan in Luke 10:25–37 demonstrates the normative command to love. In a similar manner, virtue ethics "appreciates the role that paradigmatic stories and exemplary figures play in defining particular virtues."[69]

However, when reading the story of Jesus through the lens of virtue ethics, Jesus, as the fundamental paradigm, challenges us to transform our perceptions, dispositions, and identity on the levels of vision, emotion, and character, respectively.

In his later writings, Spohn makes his claim in even stronger terms. He insists that an ethics of virtue and character that "reshapes the fundamental identity and dynamics of the person" is the most appropriate approach to Scripture.[70] It is also the most adequate approach to Scripture because it captures the relationships to Christ, God, and others that constitute the Christian way of life.

However, like Kotva, Spohn admits that Scripture plays a role in virtue ethics in return:[71] Scripture does not only exemplify the insights of virtue ethics but also brings out certain issues that are beyond the scope of philosophical ethics, which only deepens the significance of virtue ethics as a worthy hermeneutics. Thus, human sinfulness, the need of God's grace, and subsequent radical transformation (or conversion) illustrate not only the affinity between virtue ethics and Scripture but more importantly between a theologically based virtue ethics and Scripture. For example, the writers of the Synoptic Gospels depict the long, gradual process of the disciple's transformation from resisting to accepting the radical call of Jesus. Paul, in addition, emphasizes the need of God's grace in the framework of sanctification for radical conversion and moral growth. In other words, the New Testament "gives content to the formal patterns of virtue ethics" by spelling out concrete transformative habits.[72] Furthermore, Spohn claims that "when the resources of character and virtue ethics are brought to bear on biblical material, it can yield a more ethically sophisticated account of Christian experience than spirituality can offer by itself."[73]

Based on these arguments, I now turn to his reading of the New Testament through virtue ethics. However, I first offer three methodological remarks. The first is that Spohn does not handle the biblical texts in the same way Kotva does. Although he, like

Kotva, points out certain common grounds between the Gospels and virtue ethics, Spohn does not offer a comparative, cross-examination of the two to highlight their potential compatibility and connectedness. And despite occasional identification of particular virtues from the texts, such as the virtue of forgiveness in Matthew 18:21–35, he does not present us with a list of virtues either.

The second remark concerns his employment of analogical imagination.[74] Spohn claims that analogical imagination helps bridge the moral reflection of Christians and the words and deeds of Jesus, especially by providing reasons and ideas (or what he calls "cognitive content"[75]) for obeying Jesus' command to discover new ways of acting faithfully and creatively. The notion of analogy refers to "[moving] from a familiar pattern to new experience [and] looking for similarities and dissimilarities [between the prototype and the problematic situation]."[76] It implies actions and living patterns that are congruent to the prototype and, hence, have a normative value. It thus requires the presence of various cases. Among them, the paradigm case is the most important for understanding analogy; for it is a model for action. All biblical literature—including biblical rules and principles—promotes analogical reflection. The Good Samaritan, for instance, is a classic paradigm of perception and blindness.

When one discerns what to do, one engages in imagination. Imagination "spots patterns and discovers how they transfer to new contexts."[77] According to Spohn, those conjunctions, such as "likewise" and "just as," are the "copula of the imagination" that call for fitting, imaginative actions. For Spohn analogical imagination is important to Christian ethics because "Christian discipleship is grounded in a particular person conveyed to us through the particular shape of the Gospel story."[78] It helps us to discern the contemporary moral significance of the scriptural text.

The third remark is that Spohn focuses on the New Testament story of Jesus. Specifically, he perceives that the Gospels and certain Pauline writings "vividly present the story of Jesus as the norm for Christian life."[79] For instance, Paul's letter to the Philippians offers us a glimpse of how the life of Jesus affects the Christian.

These remarks ground his subsequent reading of certain New Testament texts. In his discussion of the Johannine account of Jesus washing the disciples' feet (John 13:1–20), Spohn first points out that the scene in the story acts as the prime "analogate" while our action/response is the analogue. There are different degrees of analogical imagination in one's response—from simple reenactment of the narrative to focusing on one's responsibility to having solidarity with the poor—depending on the interpreter. A rich constellation of aspects embodied in the account, such as reversal of roles and humble service, are reproduced. The image of foot washing thus becomes a springboard and guide for appropriate dispositions and actions depending on the situation. However, for Spohn, the image as a guide is not totally open-ended to those incompatible actions, such as domination or promoting privilege.

Analogical imagination spots that the logic of Christian imitation stands out throughout the letter to the Philippians: (1) the community imitates Paul who imitates Christ—out of deep emotions and affections (e.g., loyalty and gratitude) for the other; (2) imitating Christ is to be understood as the criterion for moral discernment; and (3) the call to imitation leads one to intimacy—one becomes more like Christ. Paul's own journey is analogous to the paradigm of Christ's "descent-ascent" pattern (i.e., death on the cross and resurrection as expressed in the Christological hymn in Phil 2:6–11). Since this pattern is the standard for regaining unity, the community should look to Paul as well as others in the community who imitate the paradigm.

In Romans 6, we find the same teaching to embrace the exemplary paradigm of Christ's death on the cross and resurrection. Paul specifically identifies the practice of baptism as the recapitulation of this paradigm: for Paul, every moral act in our daily Christian life is a baptismal act. It connects sin and cross, on the one side, and morality and resurrection, on the other. From there, Spohn further notes that there is an analogy in the paradigm that graphs those indicative-imperative tensions, such as:

"The death he died, he died to sin, once for all; but the life he lives, he lives to God. So you also must consider yourselves dead to sin and alive to God in Christ Jesus" (6:10–11).

In the story of Zacchaeus (Luke 19:1–10), an exercise of analogical imagination will first identify the following cases needed for reflection:[80] "Jesus' welcome to Zacchaeus" as the paradigm; "Jesus welcomes me" as the recognition; and that "I ought to welcome the outcasts accordingly" as the challenge. However, analogical reflection also reveals how Christ takes initiative and calls us to recognize "the pattern of the Christian moral life as a response to the surprising and undeserved gift of God's acceptance of us."[81] Analogical imagination further provides clues for recognizing Christ's work in our own lives and invites us to identify ourselves with the tax collector. It guides us to understand the individual call to discipleship.

Finally, an analogous imaginative reading of the story of Jesus as a whole points to the shaping of the character of individual Christians and their communities. On the level of shaping individual character, Spohn writes, "Jesus' characteristic virtues are ingredients in the gospel stories that define them."[82] When reading the story of Jesus or parables (e.g., the prodigal son in Luke 15:11–32), we need to look into how he acted and the attitude and stance he took toward others. Over time, these readings will enter into dispositional patterns. One's action inspired by these stories then leads to habitual dispositions in the heart and defines one's character. These parables further evoke emotions, such as courage and mercy, which are qualities of character as well.

On the level of shaping the character of the community, Spohn points out that "the New Testament's preferred location of moral reflection is the community of faith, not the isolated conscience; the subject of moral development is not the individual but the faithful community."[83] And New Testament practices, such as hospitality and solidarity with the poor, form the normative basis for evaluating communal moral discernment, for they are meant to build up the Body of Christ. Though incomplete and given different priorities, these virtues and practices are necessary for the faith community.

Reading the life of Jesus, as depicted by Paul, through the lens of virtue, however, points to the emphasis on the transformation of identity, which is the conscious dimension of character: Paul's own radical change of identity as recounted in Philippians 3, for example, has led him to have new perception of the self. The Philippians, likewise, are commanded to be guided by the same call Paul received, and to follow Paul's analogous example.

Taken together, reading the New Testament story of Jesus by means of analogical imagination invites us to take up the challenge to see the world as Jesus saw it; to look behind vision into the inner dynamics of the moral life (i.e., dispositions); and to attend to the Christian identity that is the root of Christian life. These challenges to one's moral psychology echo those dimensions of virtue that I introduced earlier. Indeed, although Spohn did not focus on those (potential) similarities or connections between Scripture and virtue theory, he has insightfully demonstrated a unique way of reading Scripture through the lens of virtue that engages the reader and the biblical texts on the level of ethical practice.

My Approach

These two virtue ethicists' readings of certain New Testament writings have convinced us that the theory of virtue is compatible with Scripture, and that the hermeneutics of virtue ethics is appropriate for interpreting Scripture. Their test cases, however limited they are, have also demonstrated what the interpretation of Scripture would look like in concrete from a virtue perspective. However, I would further propose a more systematic way of demonstrating how virtue ethics is relevant in reading Scripture. This proposal is based on two convictions: first, the concept of virtue can be found in Scripture;[84] second, the dimensions of virtue I have introduced above are effective hinges and reference points for relating Scripture and virtue theory.

Many Christians would note that certain writings in the Bible explicitly talk about virtues, for example, the Hebrew wisdom literature (e.g., Proverbs). Some scholars are even more expansive: following Athanasius's word that "the entire Holy Scripture is a teacher of virtues," they claim that the moral agenda found in Scripture is written in terms of virtue.[85]

Biblical scholars, like John Barton, think otherwise. They are reluctant to claim that the Bible supports an ethics of virtue (or vice versa). Rather, they observe that the term virtue is not prominent in the Bible:[86] even though the Hebrew Bible is aware of human virtues, it does not have any particular term to articulate the general idea of virtue. In the New Testament, despite those instances that occur in the lists of vices and virtues (e.g., Gal 5:22–23), the term appears only a few times. Barton, therefore, argues that the Bible is not primarily about virtue.

Most scholars who are interested in the question of Scripture and ethics are, on the contrary, inclined to virtue. Benjamin Farley, for instance, is convinced that the Bible encourages believers to venture into a biblical ethics of virtue for it contains and commends virtues and character-building motifs. He thus attempts to offer a comprehensive exploration of virtues, claiming that "no one has identified the full range of biblical virtues that support such an interest [in virtue ethics]."[87] In the Hebrew Bible, although there is no provision of a definitive list of virtues, particular virtues among certain Hebrew figures of different historical periods are found, such as Gideon's sobriety (Judges 8:23). The wisdom literature, especially, supplies us with numerous virtues, such as loyalty toward spouse and family, honesty, integrity, and faithfulness.

The New Testament is even more convincing. There are extensive lists of virtues and character-molding motifs in the texts. For example, the Beatitudes in Matthew 5 extols eight corresponding virtues, including meekness, mercy, and courage. The parables of the Synoptic Gospels also point to a variety of virtues, such as vigilance, accountability, and social consciousness (e.g., Mark 13:32–37). John's Gospel highlights the virtues of constancy, perseverance, and endurance (e.g., 15:4–5). For Paul, all virtues are set within the context of salvation by grace through faith. Consequently, besides the three theological virtues of faith, hope, and charity, Paul also calls for various virtues based on different communal contexts, such as self-control for the Galatians (5:22), renewal and humility for the Romans (12:2–3), and mutual subordination/love for the Ephesians (5:21–32).

Scripture not only reveals moral virtues, values, and vision, it actually promotes them. Specifically, as Birch and Rasmussen claim, Scripture "helps form and name virtues...and creates and renews moral vision."[88] Their claim suggests that Scripture can be relevant to virtue. Still, I further claim that the important dimensions of virtue introduced above are, in turn, hinges to relate virtue theory and Scripture.

Scripture and Character Formation

The concrete lists of virtues found in the Hebrew Bible and the New Testament and the Bible's discussion of virtues provide "a touchstone and a point of reference for theological discussions of virtues and Christian character."[89] This is because, as Lisa Sowle Cahill explains, Scripture orients the believers (on both individual and communal levels) around certain values, principles, and virtues—such as repentance, forgiveness, and compassion—that reflect God's self-revelation in Christ. Moreover, Scripture is the witness of Israel and the early Church both to their struggles to be God's faithful people (and community) and to their responses to God's revelation in concrete life experience. Whenever individuals and the faith community reflect on these life experiences recorded in Scripture, their basic character is shaped. In other words, Scripture shapes the reader's character as well as the character of the reader's community. For example, those biblical stories that narrate Jesus' associations with the outcasts and sinners, as Birch and Rasmussen rightly claim, shape the followers of Christ and their faith community into one that is inclusive and ever renewing.

Still, Scripture and its corresponding virtues not only shape our character but also our character as distinctively Christian. Scripture defines first the Christian virtues and, thereby, shapes one's character. The Judeo-Christian story provides what is needed (e.g., metaphors and concepts) for the shaping of Judeo-

Christian character. Thus, the Bible is more important in forming character than in offering explicit ethical discourse.

Scripture also acts as a shaper of Christian identity in that it is the "prime source of the self-conscious identity of the community of faith, and…of those individuals who choose to identify themselves with the church and its faith tradition."[90] Therefore, it is in relation to the Bible that the moral subject is distinctively identified as a Christian.

Scripture and Exemplar

As cited in our exploration of the goods of virtue, Hebrew biblical figures Judith, Ruth, and Naomi are examples of role models for the virtues of courage, loyalty, and love of family, respectively. Indeed, the Bible contains many "characters" that play the role of modeling for us certain moral characters. Barton, though he hesitates to claim that Scripture has any explicit idea of virtue ethics, similarly acknowledges that biblical stories (and their characters) have exemplary moral value in presenting humankind in all its singularity. For instance, the story of David presents to us not just a defective life but also an examined life that "manifests a concern for how one ought to live even when this runs clearly counter to the character's own moral insight."[91] Consequently, the Bible contributes to moral formation by telling the stories of those exemplary figures and of the community.

Sometimes, the exemplary role of the biblical figures for virtues is presented rather straightforward. In James 5:11, for example, the author explicitly calls us to imitate Job in his virtue of patience and endurance in hard times. At other times, it is not. The lack of explicit quotations, as one ethicist rightly claims, does not necessarily mean that the specific biblical text or theological insight is irrelevant.[92] Indeed, biblical figures can play the exemplary role in an implicit manner. One particular example is the virtue of hospitality exemplified in the lives of many in the Bible.

One can find detailed accounts of welcome (e.g., the welcoming of Elisha by a wealthy Shunammite woman in 2 Kgs 4) and inhospitality (e.g., the story of the men of Sodom in Gen 19 and of Gibeah in Judg 19) in the Hebrew Bible. Similarly, in the New Testament, both the Good Samaritan in Luke 10:25–37 and the person of Jesus are vivid models for practicing hospitality. However, there are others throughout. Specifically, I argue that the Hebrew Bible figure of Boaz—the husband of Ruth—in the Book of Ruth is also an exemplary figure in cultivating the virtue of hospitality: both Ruth the Moabite and the land are redeemed through his unusual and exemplary words and deeds of hospitality.[93] Still, the person of Boaz is a model of hospitality not just for individual Israelites but also for a reformed postexilic Israelite community whose *telos* is being a hospitable community.

In short, Scripture is a rich source for providing exemplary models—either explicitly or implicitly—for the cultivation of virtues and our moral formation as individuals and a faith community.

Scripture and Community/Communal Identity

Scripture is relevant not just to an individual's character formation but also to community and communal identity; for character is "a process of communal formation of individual identity."[94] This relevance is best expressed in the words of William Brown: "Scripture forms community as much as community informs the reading of Scripture."[95] Patrick Miller further rightly insists that the scriptural texts "do not speak about a *general* understanding of community but of the formation of a *particular* community whose identity as a people is evoked by their inextricable relationship to the Lord."[96] These specific communities formed by Scripture are thus diverse and historical. Moreover, Scripture does not simply form particular, historical, and diverse communities but, more importantly, *moral* communities, for moral characters are an inherent and constitutive element of a community. In this manner, as Miller and others see it, the Bible plays the role of generating and sustaining not just the community but its spiritual-moral formation as well.

Let's turn to Boaz in the Book of Ruth again. Biblical scholars agree that the main characters of the postexilic period were "dedicated to the task of reforming Israel...that she might become...nothing less than the covenant people of God."[97] Consequently, the narratives found in the books of the postexilic period are meant not merely to describe but to change the society to which the returnees belong. The writer of the Book of Ruth, therefore, in portraying the character of Boaz during the restoration period, aims at reforming and rebuilding the Israelite community into a hospitable community. The Gospels, likewise, do not simply portray a unique human being but also serve as manuals for training the follower to be part of the new community.

In sum, Scripture as narrative does not only describe the character (of God) but also "render[s] a community capable of ordering its existence [in a way] appropriate to such stories."[98] It portrays the kind of moral community to be formed and is addressed to the community. It also calls for moral reformation on the communal level. Last, but not least, Cahill rightly notes that by forming communities that are consistent with God's revelation, Scripture gains its authority in morality. The more faithful we are to the Bible, the more we recognize its authority, and hopefully, vice versa.

The above systematic presentation of the characteristics, dimensions, and issues of adaptation of virtue theory, as well as concrete instances of relating Scripture and virtue ethics, point to the worthiness of virtue theory as a hermeneutical tool in doing biblical ethics. My own approach further suggests that the four important dimensions of virtue ethics can serve as hinges and reference points in bridging the two disciplines. What remains is the practice of acquiring exegetical skill and employing a virtue framework by both biblical scholars and Christian ethicists.

CONCLUSION

FROM BRIDGE-BUILDING TO INTEGRATION AND DIALOGUE

What I have been advocating so far may be a very challenging task in the sense that it demands biblical scholars and Christian ethicists to acquire both the skill and knowledge of the other's expertise when engaging in a Scripture-based theological ethics. It may take many years before a new generation of biblical ethics scholars is trained in this fashion. What can be done during this interim period?

In the third chapter, I pointed out that several biblical scholars and theological ethicists have been trying to build the bridge through their joint writings and/or teaching, although their approaches are quite different from each other. While their joint efforts are experimental in many ways, it seems to me that it could be the right, though temporary, path within a university setting. I now briefly look at two very current, concrete examples that are found in two major universities.

When I was appointed as a Visiting Fellow at Yale Divinity School for the academic year 2010–11, two young professors, Hebrew Scripture scholar Carolyn Sharp and Christian ethicist Willis Jenkins were co-teaching in the Fall semester "an interdisciplinary seminar…that addresse[d] the relation of scriptural interpretation and Christian responses to poverty."[1] Specifically, they investigated "the intersections among Christian appropriations of biblical traditions (e.g., Deuteronomy, Amos, and Ruth) and Christian interpretations of economic justice (focusing on twentieth Century Catholic and Protestant social thought) in relation to contemporary confrontations with poverty and engagements with globalization."[2] In doing so, they first reviewed the different models of Scripture and social ethics, such as social gospel, Catholic social teaching, and liberation theology. Then, they employed these various social ethics models to interpret the selected biblical texts related to poverty.

While this was their first time of joint teaching and while they presented to us different social ethics models of reading Scripture rather than employing a specific hermeneutical tool, their efforts confirm the value of collaboration between the two disciplines and signify the growing awareness of this consensus among the younger scholars.

The second case of team teaching happened the following year. Thomist ethicist Steve Pope and Hebrew Scripture scholar David Vanderhooft, both from the Theology Department of Boston College, jointly launched—for the first time—a course entitled "God and Morality: The Ethical Legacy of the Hebrew Bible."[3] The aim of the course was to examine some major texts—such as the Ten Commandments and the Prophets—from the Hebrew Bible on selected moral issues, such as war, stealing, and lying. They began with offering exegetical analysis of these texts and, then, studied their application in the history of Christian theological ethics. They also turned to some general ethical themes, such as covenant and law, and virtues and vices for reflection.

Although the course also looked to the Hebrew Bible for insights, it differed from that of Sharp and Jenkins both in terms of content and approaches: Pope and Vanderhooft looked into more scriptural texts and engaged them with various ethical themes rather than focusing on a particular issue. They also first offered an exegesis of the text before reflecting on its ethical implications. As a result, their work was closer to that of James Keenan and Daniel Harrington, while the attempt by Sharp and Jenkins was, in part, similar to that of Richard Clifford and Thomas Massaro.

When I was teaching in the same institution where William Spohn and John Donahue had earlier taught together, a new dictionary, *Dictionary of Scripture and Ethics*, had just been launched.[4] Despite the fact that all the entries were contributed by either biblical scholars or Christian ethicists on their own, rather than coauthored, it is a long-awaited reference book and it shows how collaboration can be done (and the bridge can be built) in creative ways.

I hope that more of such collaborations between biblical scholars and Christian ethicists can be continued in the near future. But as a Catholic theological ethicist who also engages in cross-cultural dialogue within a Confucian context, I have a further desideratum: that the bridge being built can, *in the long-run*, be a model for biblical scholars and Christian ethicists together to reach out to other theological disciplines and even to ethical systems of other religions and cultures. Two possibilities emerge.

The first is the idea of integration and multidisciplinary studies. Our review and critique of Sandra Schneiders's work reveals that she is equally interested in bridging biblical studies and spirituality, especially through the Gospel of John. Spohn, in his later academic life, similarly integrated spirituality into his ethical quest, as manifested in his writings, such as "The Need for Roots and Wings: Spirituality and Christian Ethics."[5]

Still, Spohn went beyond building just another bridge and attempted to integrate biblical studies, Christian ethics, and spirituality together. In doing so, he first draws on the traditional sense of spirituality that he construes as "the practical, affective, and transformative side of authentic religion."[6] Its practices are both pedagogical and transformational, for they help train one's moral dispositions and transform one's emotions and actions that lead to embracing a more authentic way of existence. Consequently, virtue ethics and spirituality "share common ground in appreciating the formative role of habitual behavior" so that the notion of "practices" is a key to linking the two disciplines.[7] As one reviewer puts it, for Spohn, "the formation of the character of the moral agent is done through practices of spirituality."[8]

Spohn then argues that the New Testament, virtue ethics, and spirituality complement one another as sources for critical reflection on discipleship. "The story of Jesus," he says, "shapes

Christian ethics through the convergence of…the New Testament, virtue ethics, and spirituality."[9] The complementary relationship among them can be summarized as follows. First, New Testament and virtue ethics together move spirituality beyond what is private and descriptive to the normative. The communal aspect of virtue, for example, checks one's inclination to use spirituality solely as an instrument for self-enhancement. Virtue ethics also draws out the implications of the spiritual practices and rituals.

Second, both spirituality and virtue theory emphasize personal engagement in such a way that it can be beneficial for the exegetical task (by inviting the exegete to go beyond textual criticism). Together they appropriate a more complete moral vision of Jesus, for the New Testament aims at transforming not only our external actions but also our inner hearts. Moreover, virtue ethics, likewise, draws out the implications of the biblical symbols while spirituality spells out practices that nurture the habits of mind.

Third, the New Testament and spirituality are important means to persuade the faithful to commit themselves to their moral goals: the New Testament provides definite content to our moral life and an alternative format (e.g., narratives) that assist us to better grasp the intrinsic meaning of ethical norms. As discussed above, it also raises issues that are not treated in philosophical ethics, such as grace and sin. Spirituality further spells out practices that nurture the habits of the heart.

Another sign of integration is found in the work of French theologian Louis-Marie Chauvet. When Chauvet explores the sacraments in the symbolic network of the faith of the Church, he turns to the individual relationships that sacramental theology has with both Scripture and ethics.[10] He notes that they are not two isolated pairs of mutual relationships but that there exists integration (albeit tensions) among biblical studies, ethics, and sacramental theology.

Regarding the relationship between Scripture and sacraments, there is "a sacramentality of Scripture, and inversely… Scripture opens up sacramentality from the inside."[11] The proclamation of the Word in a liturgy is the sacramental manifestation of the essence of the Bible. The relationship between sacraments and ethics, in contrast, is characterized by an evangelical tension between ritual and ethical practices. Yet, corporality, which is "the primordial location of the Christian liturgy" on the one hand, and "the theological import of an ethics lived as the prime place of a liturgy" on the other, becomes the meeting place of the two.[12] Moreover, sacrament serves as a symbol for the ongoing passage from the text toward the body.

As a whole, Chauvet perceives them as the three elements that form the structure of Christian identity. They are linked in the symbolic mediation of the Church and can be understood as a fundamental anthropological structure of cognition-recognition-praxis.[13]

The second possibility points to interfaith and cross-cultural dialogues. Methodologically speaking, many major religions and traditions, such as Confucianism, go to the texts in their search of ethical teachings, that is, their ethics are primarily the fruit of careful interpretation of their "sacred" texts. Now that I have been arguing for greater attentiveness to the scriptural text throughout my advocacy for a more integrated, Scripture-based Christian ethics, common grounds are thus created that can be helpful to make Christian ethics, as such, more explicable to other religious communities, and more supportive of interfaith and cross-cultural dialogues with their ethics. For doing an interfaith or cross-cultural ethics begins not with analogous generalities but very specific texts, and needs to be both text-based and interpretative.

A proposed example is how the Decalogue (Exod 5:2–17) and the Beatitudes (Matt 5:3–12) as "scripted script" can be compared to the virtues of the Confucian tradition, and made meaningful to its Confucian Chinese audience. By turning to the sacred texts of the Confucian tradition and extracting their moral virtues, I note that they match those of the Decalogue and the Beatitudes in many positive areas.[14]

Let me take the second beatitude as an illustration. A careful exegesis shows that those who are sensitive toward and mourn over the suffering of the poor demonstrate that mourning is an expression of the virtue of solidarity. It calls for our awareness of the suffering in the world, protest against social injustice, and reflection on our personal, communal, and social practices.

Although the concept of solidarity is not explicitly found in the Confucian tradition, stories of mourning and ritual practices of mourning can be identified in the writings of some major figures of the classical period of Confucianism. For instance, in the *Analects* we find, "When Yen Yuan died, the Master [Confucius] said, 'Alas! Heaven has bereft me! Heaven has bereft me!'"[15] Mencius (who is said to be a student of Confucius's grandson) suggested that sensitivity toward the sufferer is an innate response of humankind. He thus said, "No man is devoid of a heart sensitive to the suffering of others."[16] Xunzi (a contemporary figure to Mencius), who stressed the importance of the virtue of ritual propriety, perceived mourning as, not just a proper ritual practice to express due reverence and grief, but that it has practical and social purpose as well—it distinguishes the duties owed to different people and prevents forgetfulness; moreover, it represents the ultimate principle of harmony and unity within a community.[17]

With regards to being in solidarity with the sufferer, Confucius pointed out that the first step is to empathize with the sufferer. For example, he said, "When eating in the presence of one who had been bereaved, the Master never ate his full."[18] Although it is the belief of the Confucian tradition that *chün tzu,* one who has fully developed his moral nature, would understand this ultimate mystery of suffering and accept it willingly, it is also the common belief of Confucian thinkers that one's moral nature commits the person to accompany and help others to understand and ease their suffering. It is a moral responsibility of the moral person.[19]

I am convinced that a comparative exercise of this sort can provide an opportunity to demonstrate another possible benefit, resulting from the methodological shift to a more integrated Scripture-based ethics, and throw light on this future direction—one that is more capable of interfaith and cross-cultural exchange.

NOTES

Foreword

1. Interestingly, he could have included himself. See his own work, Yiu Sing Lúcás Chan, *The Ten Commandments and the Beatitudes: Biblical Studies and Ethics in Real Life* (Lanham, MD: Rowman and Littlefield Publishers, 2012).

Preface

1. William C. Spohn, *What Are They Saying about Scripture and Ethics?* fully revised and expanded ed. (Mahwah, NJ: Paulist Press, 1995).

2. ibid., 8.

Introduction

1. In this book, the term "Scripture" is used interchangeably with "Bible" and refers to those sacred writings that the Christian community considers "canonical," or authoritative for belief and practice.

2. Luke Timothy Johnson, "The Bible's Authority for and in the Church," in *Engaging Biblical Authority: Perspectives on the Bible as Scripture,* ed. William P. Brown (Louisville, KY: Westminster John Knox Press, 2007), 62. In this brief account on the development within the Catholic tradition, I consulted the following works: James T. Bretzke, *A Morally Complex World. Engaging Contemporary Moral Theology* (Collegeville, MN: Liturgical Press, 2004); Charles E. Curran, "The Role and Function of the Scriptures in Moral Theology," in *Readings in Moral Theology No. 4.*

The Use of Scripture in Moral Theology, ed. Charles Curran and Richard McCormick (New York: Paulist Press, 1984), 178–212; *The Catholic Moral Tradition Today: A Synthesis* (Washington, DC: Georgetown University Press, 1999); Pontifical Biblical Commission, *The Bible and Morality: Biblical Roots of Christian Conduct* (Vatican: Libreria Editrice Vaticana, 2008); William C. Spohn, "Scripture," in *The Oxford Handbook of Theological Ethics*, ed. Gilbert Meilaender and William Werpehowski (London: Oxford University Press, 2005), 93–111.

3. Bretzke, *A Morally Complex World*, 19. Richard Gula comments that a concrete example is Gerald Kelly's use of the story of Onan in his 1950s book *Medico-Morals*. See Gula's *Reason Informed by Faith: Foundations of Catholic Morality* (New York: Paulist Press, 1989), 116.

4. Philippe Delhaye, "Le theologie morale d'hier et d'aujourd'hui," *Revue des sciences religieuses* 27 (1953): 112–30, as cited in John C. Ford and Gerald Kelly, *Contemporary Moral Theology*, vol. 1, *Questions in Fundamental Moral Theology* (Westminster, MD: The Newman Press, 1964), 47–48.

5. Vatican II, *Optatam Totius*, Decree on priestly training, October 1965, http://www.vatican.va/archive/hist_councils/ii_vatican_council/documents/vat-ii_decree_19651028_optatam-totius_en.html.

6. Daniel J. Harrington and James F. Keenan, *Jesus and Virtue Ethics: Building Bridges between New Testament Studies and Moral Theology* (Chicago, IL: Sheed & Ward, 2002), 13. The following works were consulted in this short account on the reality and the views of those who were engaged in the area of Scripture and ethics before and during the 1980s: Robert J. Daly et al., *Christian Biblical Ethics: From Biblical Revelation to Contemporary Christian Praxis* (New York: Paulist Press, 1984); Paulinus Ikechukwu Odozor, *Moral Theology in an Age of Renewal* (Notre Dame, IN: University of Notre Dame Press, 2003); Thomas W. Ogletree, *The Use of the Bible in Christian Ethics: A Constructive Essay* (Philadelphia, PA: Fortress, 1983); Pheme Perkins, "New Testament Ethics: Questions and Contexts," *Religious Studies Review* 10 (October 1984): 321–27; Sandra M. Schneiders, "From Exegesis to Hermeneutics: The Problem of the Contemporary

Meaning of Scripture," *Horizons: Journal of the College Theology Society* 8 (Spring 1981): 23–39.

7. Ogletree, *The Use of the Bible*, xi.

8. James M. Gustafson, "The Place of Scripture in Christian Ethics: A Methodological Study," *Interpretation* 24, no. 4 (October 1970): 430.

9. Edouard Hamel, "Scripture, the Soul of Moral Theology?" in *Readings in Moral Theology, No. 4. The Use of Scripture in Moral Theology*, ed. Charles E. Curran and Richard A. McCormick (New York: Paulist Press, 1984), 120–21.

10. Odozor, *Moral Theology*, 159–60. Odozor quotes the words of McCormick said during an interview.

11. Pheme Perkins, "A Note to the Reader," in *Love Commands in the New Testament* (New York: Paulist Press, 1982).

12. Harrington and Keenan, *Jesus and Virtue Ethics*, 13.

13. The data is based on their issues published between 1989 and 2009.

14. Allen Verhey, "Scripture as Script and as Scripted: The Beatitudes," in *Character Ethics and the New Testament: Moral Dimensions of Scripture*, ed. Robert L. Brawley (Louisville, KY: Westminster John Knox, 2007), 19–25.

15. Edmund Pellegrino and David Thomasma, *The Christian Virtues in Medical Practice* (Washington, DC: Georgetown University Press, 1996), 14–15.

16. William C. Spohn, *Go and Do Likewise: Jesus and Ethics* (New York: Continuum, 2000), 27–28.

Chapter 1: The Attempts by Scripture Scholars

1. For a variety of reasons, I limit my study to New Testament ethics. The first is simply because the study of methodology requires us to focus our claims: an exhaustive study of the entire Bible will not make my claims any more compelling. Second, as Hays rightly claims, the Old Testament is often "to be read through the hermeneutical lens of the New." Third, the discipline of New Testament theology itself has gone through certain developments in the past few decades, which affect our understanding of New

Testament ethics. Fourth, as an experimental work, and while not ignoring the Old Testament, I acknowledge that there are foreseeable difficulties in dealing with Old Testament ethics. See Richard B. Hays, "New Testament Ethics. A Theological Task," *Annual of the Society of Christian Ethics* (1995): 100. For an overview of the developments in New Testament theology, see Harrington and Keenan, *Jesus and Virtue Ethics*, 9; Kavin Rowe, "New Testament Theology: The Revival of a Discipline," *Journal of Biblical Literature* 125 (2006): 393–410; and Frank J. Matera, "New Testament Theology: History, Method, and Identity," *Catholic Biblical Quarterly* 67, no. 1 (January 2005): 5. For a summary of the problems that scholars of Old Testament ethics face, see John Barton, *Understanding Old Testament Ethics* (Louisville, KY: Westminster John Knox, 2003), 2–3.

2. For a discussion of the advantages and disadvantages of these two classical methods, see Eduard Lohse, *Theological Ethics of the New Testament*, trans. M. Eugene Boring (Minneapolis, MN: Fortress Press, 1991), 4–5.

3. Harrington and Keenan, *Jesus and Virtue Ethics*, 20–23; Perkins, "New Testament Ethics," 322–25.

4. Robert J. Daly, review of *The Ethics of the New Testament*, by Wolfgang Schrage, *Theological Studies* 50, no.1 (March 1989): 173.

5. Lohse, *Theological Ethics of the New Testament*, 3–4; Pheme Perkins, *Love Commands in the New Testament* (New York: Paulist Press, 1982), 1.

6. James M. Gustafson, "The Place of Scripture in Christian Ethics: A Methodological Study," *Interpretation* 24, no. 4 (October 1970): 431; Harrington and Keenan, *Jesus and Virtue Ethics*, 17–18.

7. J. Leslie Houlden, *Ethics and the New Testament*, rev. ed. (Edinburgh: T&T Clark, 1992), Introduction.

8. Ibid.

9. See James T. Bretzke, *Bibliography on Scripture and Christian Ethics* (Lewiston, ME: E. Mellen Press, 1997), 105–223.

10. See Luke Timothy Johnson, *The Literary Function of Possessions in Luke-Acts* (Missoula, MT: Scholars Press, 1977).

11. One of the earlier works written in a comprehensive style is Rudolf Schnackenburg's *The Moral Teaching of the New Testament,* first published in German in 1962 and translated into English in 1965 (Seabury Press). Another important work is Heinz-Dietrich Wendland's *Ethik des Neuen Testaments* (Vandenhoeck & Ruprecht, 1970) published a few years later. See Bretzke, *Bibliography,* 127, 133. See also Jack T. Sanders, *Ethics in the New Testament* (London: S.C.M. Press Ltd, 1976).

12. In this section, I have consulted the following reviews: James T. Bretzke, *Theology Today* 55, no. 1 (April 1998): 97–98; Richard A. Burridge, "A New Testament Ethics for South Africa," *Journal of Theology for Southern Africa* 102 (November 1998): 71–73; David Herbert, *Modern Believing* 39, no. 3 (July 1998): 55–59; Luke Timothy Johnson, *Commonweal* 124 (June 6, 1997): 23–25; Frank J. Matera, *Theological Studies* 58 (September 1997): 537–39; James I. H. McDonald, *Studies in World Christianity* 4, no. 2 (1998): 277–79; Harrington and Keenan, *Jesus and Virtue Ethics,* 21; Donald Senior, *Bible Today* 36 (March 1998): 134; Freeman Sleeper, *Interpretation* 52, no. 2 (April 1998): 200–202; William C. Spohn, "Is There Such a Thing as New Testament Ethics?" *Christian Century* 114, no. 17 (May 1997): 525–31; Walter J. Woods, *America* 177 (August 16–23, 1997): 25–26; Richard Alan Young, *Journal of the Evangelical Theological Society* 42, no. 1 (March 1999): 136–38.

Two articles of Hays other than *The Moral Vision of New Testament* (San Francisco, CA: HaperCollins, 1996) are also examined: "Scripture-shaped Community: The Problem of Method in New Testament Ethics," *Interpretation* 44, no. 1 (January 1990): 42–55; and "New Testament Ethics. A Theological Task," 97–120.

13. Hays, "Scripture-shaped Community," 43.

14. Ibid., 45.

15. Hays, "New Testament Ethics," 102; Waynes A. Meeks, "A Hermeneutics of Social Embodiment," *Harvard Theological Review* 79 (1986): 176–86, as cited in Hays, 120.

16. Hays thinks that the descriptive task is only the starting point of his entire project. He thus clarifies that he is not interested in presenting an exhaustive account of the ethical contents.

17. Senior, review of *The Moral Vision,* 134.

18. Young, review of *The Moral Vision*, 137.

19. The works of Matera that are reviewed include: *New Testament Ethics: The Legacies of Jesus and Paul* (Louisville, KY: Westminster John Knox, 1996); "Matthew 27:11–54," *Interpretation* 38, no. 1 (January 1984): 55–59; "The Death of Jesus According to Luke: A Question of Sources," *Catholic Biblical Quarterly* 47 (July 1985): 469–85; "Responsibility for the Death of Jesus according to the Acts of the Apostles," *Journal for the Study of the New Testament* 39 (June 1990): 77–93; "Ethics for the Kingdom of God: The Gospel according to Mark," *Louvain Studies* 20, no. 2–3 (Summer–Fall 1995): 187–200; "Galatians and the Development of Paul's Teaching on Justification," *Word & World* 20, no. 3 (Summer 2000): 239–48; "Christ in the Theologies of Paul and John," *Theological Studies* 67, no. 2 (June 2006): 237–56.

The following reviews are consulted: James L. Bailey, *Currents in Theology and Mission* 25, no. 1 (Fall 1998): 61–62; Brian K. Blount, *Bible Review* 13, no. 3 (June 1997): 116–20; David G. Horrell, *Theology* 100, no. 797 (September–October 1997): 383; Andrew T. Lincoln, *Pro Ecclesia* 8, no. 1 (Winter 1999): 118–20; Chris McMahon, *Living Light* 36 (January 2001): 70–74; Stephen Pattee, *Catholic Biblical Quarterly* 60, no. 2 (April 1998): 370–71; Sandra Hack Polaski, *Review & Expositor* 95, no. 1 (Winter 1998): 119; Freeman Sleeper, *Interpretation* 52, no. 2 (April 1998): 200–202; John Topel, *Theological Studies* 58, no. 4 (December 1997): 723–24; Jozef Verheyden, *Louvain Studies* 23, no. 1 (Spring 1998): 79–80; Walter J. Woods, *America* 177 (August 16–23, 1997): 25–26; Richard Alan Young, *Journal of the Evangelical Theological Society* 42, no. 2 (June 1999): 342–44.

20. Matera, "Ethics for the Kingdom of God," 187. See also 195–200.

21. The other two works of his trilogy are: *Passion Narratives and Gospel Theologies* (1986) and *New Testament Christology* (1999). In 2007, he published *New Testament Theology*, which offers a better treatment of the kingdom of God theme.

22. McMahon, review of *New Testament Ethics*, 71.

23. Young, review of *New Testament Ethics*, 343.

24. Ibid.

25. Matera, *New Testament Ethics*, 7.

26. For example, Johannine writings contain many of the themes found in the Synoptics, but they develop these themes in a new way.

27. There are over 20 reviews written in English and Spanish.

28. Lincoln, review of *New Testament Ethics*, 120.

29. Pattee, review of *New Testament Ethics*, 371.

30. A small trace of a hermeneutic stance can be found: for example, in his treatment of homosexuality in Romans 1, see Matera, *New Testament Ethics*, 293 n. 16. For other similar examples, see also 223–27.

31. Pattee tries to explain that the issue of slavery in Philemon is treated as part of the household code of Ephesians and Colossians. However, the treatment is extremely brief.

32. In this section, the following reviews are consulted: William Baird, *Encounter* 54, no. 1 (Winter 1993): 92–94; Karen A. Barta, *Theological Studies* 54, no. 1 (March 1993): 165–66; Mary C. Boys, *Cross Currents* 42, no. 2 (Summer 1992): 246–50; Michael Cahill, *Theology Today* 49, no. 3 (October 1992): 414–16; Kathryn Greene-McCreight, *Journal of Religion* 74, no. 1 (January 1994): 93; Anthony D. Hopkins, *Review & Expositor* 90, no. 1 (Winter 1993): 136–37; Lewis Seymour Mudge, *Christian Century* 109, no. 27 (September 23–30, 1992): 848–49; Donald Senior, *Catholic Biblical Quarterly* 55, no. 3 (July 1993): 609–10.

Several of Schneiders's works are examined as well. See *The Revelatory Text: Interpreting the New Testament as Sacred Scripture* (Collegeville, MN: Liturgical Press, 1991, 2nd edition 1999); *Written That You May Believe: Encountering Jesus in the Fourth Gospel* (New York: Crossroad Publishing, 1999); "Faith, Hermeneutics, and the Literal Sense of Scripture," *Theological Studies* 39, no. 4 (December 1978): 719–36; "The Paschal Imagination: Objectivity and Subjectivity in New Testament Interpretation," *Theological Studies* 43 (March 1982): 52–68; "New Testament Reflections on Peace and Nuclear Arms," in *Catholics and Nuclear War: A Commentary on the Challenge of Peace, the U.S. Catholic Bishops' Pastoral Letter on War and Peace*, ed. Philip J. Murnion (New York: Crossroad Publishing Co., 1983), 91–105; "Church and Biblical Scholarship in Dialogue," *Theology Today* 42, no. 3 (October 1985): 353–58; "John 20:11–18: The Encounter of the Easter Jesus with

Mary Magdalene—A Transformative Feminist Reading," in *What Is John? Readers and Readings of the Fourth Gospel*, ed. Fernando F. Segovia (Atlanta, GA: Scholars Press, 1996), 155–58.

33. Schneiders, *The Revelatory Text*, 3.

34. Ibid., 4.

35. Schneiders, "From Exegesis to Hermeneutics," 27.

36. Ibid., 33–34.

37. Schneiders, *The Revelatory Text*, 13.

38. Schneiders, "New Testament Reflections," 94.

39. Schneiders, *The Revelatory Text*, 127.

40. Cahill, review of *The Revelatory Text*, 415.

41. Schneiders, *The Revelatory Text*, 120–21, 171.

42. Unfortunately, in both works, the whole biblical canon is employed to support her discussion of specific Johannine texts.

43. Schneiders, *Written That You May Believe*, 5.

44. The following articles and works of Sugirtharajah are examined: *Asian Biblical Hermeneutics and Postcolonialism: Contesting the Interpretations* (Sheffield: Sheffield Academic Press, 1999); *The Bible and the Third World: The Precolonial, Colonial and Postcolonial Encounters* (New York: Cambridge University Press, 2001); *Postcolonial Criticism and Biblical Interpretation* (New York: Oxford University Press, 2002); "Introduction, and Some Thoughts on Asian Biblical Hermeneutics," *Biblical Interpretation* 2, no. 3 (1994): 251–63; "Introduction: Empires Old and New," in *The Postcolonial Biblical Reader*, ed. Rasiah S. Sugirtharajah (Malden, MA: Blackwell, 2006), 67–68; "The First, Second and Third Letters of John," in *A Postcolonial Commentary on the New Testament Writings*, ed. Fernando Segovia and Rasiah S. Sugirtharajah (New York: T&T Clark, 2007), 413–23.

Other reviews and writings consulted include: Colin Morris, *Heythrop Journal* 42, no. 3 (July 2001): 354–55; George Pixley, *Journal of the American Academy of Religion* 71, no. 4 (December 2003): 973–75; Bonnie Roos, *Journal of Biblical Literature* 122, no. 4 (Winter 2003): 745–51; Christopher Rowland, *Journal of Theological Studies* 52, no. 2 (October 2001): 863–64; Khiok-khng Yeo, *Catholic Biblical Quarterly* 62, no. 1 (January 2000): 166–68; and Pui-lan Kwok, "Making the Connections: Postcolonial Studies and Feminist Biblical Interpretation," in *The Postcolonial*

Biblical Reader, ed. Rasiah S. Sugirtharajah (Malden, MA: Blackwell, 2006), 45–63.

45. I follow Sugirtharajah in the use of the term "Third World" in that it is used in a rehabilitated sense rather than in a negative or geographical sense.

46. Fernando F. Segovia, *Decolonizing Biblical Studies: A View from the Margins* (Maryknoll, NY: Orbis Books, 2000), 121–22, as cited in Kwok, "Making the Connections," 46.

47. Sugirtharajah, *Postcolonial Criticism*, 21.

48. Sugirtharajah, *Asian Biblical Hermeneutics*, 18–19.

49. Sugirtharajah borrows the decoding scheme from Stuart Hall. See Stuart Hall, *Encoding and Decoding in the Television Discourse* (Birmingham: Centre for Cultural Studies, University of Birmingham, 1973), 16–18.

50. Sugirtharajah, "Introduction: Empires Old and New," 67. See also Jon L. Berquist, "Postcolonialism and Imperial Motives for Canonization," in *The Postcolonial Biblical Reader*, ed. Rasiah S. Sugirtharajah (Malden, MA: Blackwell, 2006), 78–95.

51. Sugirtharajah, *The Bible and the Third World*, 257–58.

52. Ibid., 272.

Chapter 2: The Attempts by Theological Ethicists

1. See Kenneth Himes, "Scripture and Ethics: A Review Essay," *Biblical Theology Bulletin* 15, no. 2 (1985): 65–73; William C. Spohn, "The Use of Scripture in Moral Theology," *Theological Studies* 47, no. 1 (1986): 88–102. These four tasks echo the four major aspects identified by Curran and McCormick. See Charles E. Curran and Richard A. McCormick, eds., *Readings in Moral Theology, No. 4. The Use of Scripture in Moral Theology* (New York: Paulist Press, 1984), vii–viii.

2. For a discussion of "revealed morality" and "revealed reality," see Gustafson, "The Place of Scripture," 439, 441–45.

3. The tensions between Scripture and the other three sources have been recognized for a long time. See Hays, "Scripture-shaped Community," 50–51.

4. See Johnson, "The Bible's Authority," 65–66; Lisa Sowle Cahill, "The Bible and Ethics: Hermeneutical Dilemmas," in *Between the Sexes: Foundations for a Christian Ethics of Sexuality* (Philadelphia, PA: Fortress Press, 1985), 5, and "The New Testament and Ethics: Communities of Social Change," *Interpretation* 44, no. 4 (October 1990): 384.

5. Daly et al., *Christian Biblical Ethics*, 68. See also Bruce C. Birch and Larry L. Rasmussen, *Bible and Ethics in Christian Life*, rev. ed. (Minneapolis, MN: Augsburg, 1989), 153–55.

6. Birch and Rasmussen, *Bible and Ethics in Christian Life*, 141–43.

7. Cahill, "The Bible and Ethics," 23.

8. Himes, "Scripture and Ethics," 71–72.

9. See James F. Childress, "Scripture and Christian Ethics: Some Reflections on the Role of Scripture in Moral Deliberation and Justification," *Interpretation* 34, no. 4 (October 1980): 380; Lisa Sowle Cahill, "Canon, Authority, Norms? Recent Studies in Biblical Ethics," review of *The Great Reversal: Ethics and the New Testament*, by Allen Verhey, *Interpretation* 40, no. 4 (October 1986): 414.

10. See Spohn, "Is There Such a Thing," 525; Curran, *The Catholic Moral Tradition Today*, 49–50; Harrington and Keenan, *Jesus and Virtue Ethics*, 12; Gustafson, "The Place of Scripture," 444; Johnson, "The Bible's Authority," 68; Ogletree, *The Use of the Bible*, 177–79.

11. See Curran, *The Catholic Moral Tradition Today*, 49–50; Johnson, "The Bible's Authority," 68; Harrington and Keenan, *Jesus and Virtue Ethics*, 12; Himes, "Scripture and Ethics," 66.

12. Johannes Reiter, "Die Katholische Moraltheologie zwischen den Beiden Vatikanischen Konzils," in *Die Katholisch-theologische Disziplinen in Deutschland 1870–1962. Ihre Geschichte, ihre Zeitbezug*, ed. Hubert Wolf (Paderborn: Schöningh, 1999), 231–42. See also James F. Keenan, *A History of Catholic Moral Theology in the Twentieth Century* (New York: Continuum, 2010), 59–82.

13. Gustafson, "The Place of Scripture," 431.

14. In his *Scripture and Ethics. Twentieth-Century Portraits*, Jeffrey Siker explores how some significant contemporary

Christian ethicists have actually made use of Scripture in their own areas of interest. Among them are Häring, Gutiérrez, and Ruether. Although my focus is different, in my review of these three particular Christian ethicists, I am in debt to his work. See Jeffrey S. Siker, *Scripture and Ethics. Twentieth-Century Portraits* (New York: Oxford University Press, 1997), chaps. 4, 7, 9.

15. Apart from Siker's above-mentioned work, I also consult the following works: Ann Agnew, "Bernard Häring." http://www.shc.edu/theolibrary/resources/haring.htm; Vincent MacNamara, *Faith and Ethics: Recent Roman Catholicism* (Washington, DC: Georgetown University Press, 1985); James F. Keenan, "Bernard Häring's Influence on American Catholic Moral Theology," *Journal of Moral Theology* 1, no.1 (2012): 23–42.

The two major works of Häring as well as a couple of his articles on Scripture are also explored: *Das Gesetz Christi. Moraltheologie für Priester und Laien* (Freiburg: Erich Wewel Verlag, 1954); *The Law of Christ*, 3 vols., trans. Edwin Kaiser (Westminster, MD: Newman Press, 1961, 1963, 1966); *Free and Faithful in Christ: Moral Theology for Clergy and Laity*, 3 vols. (New York: Seabury Press/Crossroad, 1978, 1979, 1981); "The Normative Value of the Sermon on the Mount." *Catholic Biblical Quarterly* 29 (1967): 69–79; "The Role of the Catholic Moral Theologian," in *Moral Theology: Challenges for the Future*, ed. Richard A. McCormick, Charles E. Curran, and Walter J. Burghardt (Mahwah, NJ: Paulist Press, 1990), 32–47.

16. Curran, "The Role and Function of the Scriptures," 180.

17. Häring, *The Law of Christ*, 1:viii.

18. Häring, *Free and Faithful in Christ*, 1:6.

19. Charles E. Curran, "Bernard Häring: A Moral Theologian Whose Soul Matched His Scholarship," *National Catholic Reporter* 34 (July 17, 1998): 11.

20. Häring, *Free and Faithful in Christ*, 1:23–24.

21. Ibid., 1:6.

22. Siker notes that the ethics of response permeates Häring's approach to both moral theology and Scripture.

23. Häring, *Free and Faithful in Christ*, 1:307.

24. Ibid., 1:139.

25. Ibid., 1:334.

26. Ibid., 1:331.

27. Siker, *Scripture and Ethics*, 78.

28. The following works and reviews are consulted here: William B. Duncan, *The Political Philosophy of Peruvian Theologian Gustavo Gutiérrez*, Toronto Studies in Theology, vol. 85 (New York: Edwin Mellen Press, 2001); Thomas L. Schubeck, *Liberation Ethics: Sources, Models, and Norms* (Minneapolis, MN: Fortress Press, 1993); John W. de Gruchy, *Journal of Theology for Southern Africa* 68 (Spring 1989): 119; Pierre Hegy, *Journal for the Scientific Study of Religion* 13, no. 2 (June 1974): 243–44; Paul R. Raabe, *Concordia Journal* 15, no. 2 (April 1989): 211–12.

The major works of Gutiérrez that are specifically explored include: *On Job: God-Talk and the Suffering of the Innocent*, trans. Matthew J. O'Connell (Maryknoll, NY: Orbis Books, 1987); *A Theology of Liberation*, 2nd ed., trans. and ed. Sister Caridad Inda and John Eagelson (Maryknoll, NY: Orbis Books, 1988); *The Truth Shall Make You Free* (Maryknoll, NY: Orbis Books, 1990); *God of Life* (Maryknoll, NY: Orbis Books, 1991).

29. Schubeck, *Liberation Ethics*, 152.

30. Gutiérrez, *The Truth Shall Make You Free*, 47–48.

31. John P. Meier, "The Bible as Source of Theology," *CTSA Proceedings* 43 (1988): 1–3.

32. Gutiérrez, *A Theology of Liberation*, xxix.

33. Ibid., xiv, xxvii.

34. Gustavo Gutiérrez, "Freedom and Salvation," in *Liberation and Change*, ed. Ronald H. Stone (Atlanta, GA: John Knox Press, 1977), 90. See also Anthony J. Tambasco, "First and Third World Ethics," in *Christian Biblical Ethics: From Biblical Revelation to Contemporary Christian Praxis*, ed. Robert J. Daly et al. (New York: Paulist Press, 1984), 139–42.

35. See Gustavo Gutiérrez, "The Irruption of the Poor in Latin America and the Christian Communities of the Common People," in *The Challenge of Basic Christian Communities*, ed. Sergio Torres and John Eagleson, trans. John Drury (Maryknoll, NY: Orbis Books, 1981), 121.

36. Schubeck, *Liberation Ethics*, 161.

37. See Congregation for the Doctrine of the Faith, "Ten Observations on the Theology of Gustavo Gutiérrez," in *Liberation*

Theology: A Documentary History, ed. Alfred T. Hennelly (Maryknoll, NY: Orbis Books, 1990), 348–50. The statement was first published in March 1983. The English text was translated by Hennelly from the French version that Hennelly obtained in 1984. Hennelly claims that the little publicity given to the statement by the Congregation implies that its interpretation of Gutiérrez's theology is incorrect.

38. The survey here focuses on the some of the more recent works of Ruether: *Sexism and God-Talk* (Boston, MA: Beacon Press, 1983); *Disputed Questions: On Being a Christian* (Maryknoll, NY: Orbis Books, 1989); *Gaia and God: An Ecofeminist Theology of Earth Healing* (San Francisco, CA: HarperSanFrancisco, 1994); "Feminism and Patriarchal Religion: Principles of Ideological Critique of the Bible," *Journal for the Study of the Old Testament* 22 (Fall 1982): 54–66; "Feminist Interpretation: A Method of Correlation," in *Feminist Interpretation of the Bible*, ed. Letty M. Russell (Philadelphia, PA: Westminster, 1985), 111–24; "The Future of Feminist Theology," *Journal of the American Academy of Religion* 53, no. 4 (December 1985): 703–13; "Feminist Hermeneutics, Scriptural Authority, and Religious Experience: The Case of the *Imago Dei* and Gender Equality," in *Radical Pluralism and Truth*, ed. Werner G. Jeanrond and Jennifer L. Rike (New York: Crossroad, 1991), 95–106; "Imago Dei, Christian Tradition and Feminist Hermeneutics," in *Image of God and Gender Models in Judaeo-Christian Tradition*, ed. Kari Elizabeth Børresen (Oslo: Solum Forlag, 1991), 258–81. Although some of these works were written over 25 years ago, the fact that they have been reprinted again in the past fifteen years affirms their ongoing value in the discussion of feminist hermeneutics.

Other works and reviews consulted here include: Angela V. Askew, *Union Seminary Quarterly Review* 40, no. 3 (1985): 59–68; Rebecca S. Chopp, "Seeing and Naming the World Anew: The Works of Rosemary Radford Ruether," *Religious Studies Review* 15, no. 1 (January 1989): 8–11; Regina Coll, *Religious Education* 79, no. 1 (Winter 1984): 135–37; James W. Fowler, *Christian Century* 100, no. 30 (October 19, 1983): 940–41; Rosalind F. Hinton, "A Legacy of Inclusion: An Interview with Rosemary Radford Ruether," *Cross Currents* 52, no. 1 (Spring 2002): 28–37; Winsome

Munro, *Religious Education* 78, no. 4 (Fall 1983): 596–98; June O'Connor, *Religious Studies Review* 12, no. 3–4 (July–October 1986): 202–5.

39. Ruether points out that her feminist critique embraces gender, class, and race critiques, and, thus, is different from the works of other feminist scholars like Mary Daly.

40. See her *Mary: The Feminine Face of the Church* (Philadelphia, PA: The Westminster Press, 1977), 12.

41. Siker, *Scripture and Ethics*, 171.

42. Ruether, *Sexism and God-Talk*, 23.

43. Ruether, "Feminist Hermeneutics," 96.

44. I depend on Siker for the outline of the different traditions presented here.

45. Ruether, *Mary*, 40.

46. For a discussion of the various stances of this correlation, see Ruether, "Feminist Interpretation," 117–18.

47. Ruether, *Sexism and God-Talk*, 31; "Feminist Interpretation," 122.

48. Ruether, *Sexism and God-Talk*, 24.

49. It is important to note that most commentators and reviewers have commented on her feminist theology rather than her use of Scripture. Also, those who have done so are mainly Christian feminist scholars, such as Elisabeth Schüssler Fiorenza.

50. Elisabeth Schüssler Fiorenza, *In Memory of Her: A Feminist Theological Reconstruction of Christian Origins* (New York: Crossroad, 1983), 19. In a response to Fiorenza's criticism, Ruether clarifies that she is aware of the limitations of the prophetic-liberating traditions, and she was simply describing "a certain liberating 'dynamic' which is expressed in the prophetic messianic tradition." Rosemary Radford Ruether, review of *In Memory of Her: A Feminist Theological Reconstruction of Christian Origins*, by Elisabeth Schüssler Fiorenza, *Horizons* 1, no. 2 (1984): 148. See also *Sexism and God-Talk*, 33–34. In return, she is convinced that Fiorenza's approach is similar to her own.

51. Fiorenza, *In Memory of Her*, 19.

52. Carol P. Christ, "A Spirituality for Women," in *Laughter of Aphrodite: Reflections on a Journey to the Goddess* (San Francisco, CA: Harper & Row, 1987), 62–63. See also Elizabeth Achtemeier, "The

Impossible Possibility: Evaluating the Feminist Approach to Bible and Theology," *Interpretation* 42, no. 1 (January 1988): 49.

53. Gunnlaugur Jónsson, *The Image of God: Gen. 1:26–28 in a Century of Old Testament Research* (Stockholm: Almquist and Wiksell, 1988), as cited in Ruether, "Imago Dei," 262.

54. Phyllis Bird, "Male and Female, He Created Them: Gen. 1:27b in the Context of the Priestly Account of Creation," *Harvard Theological Review* 74 (1981): 128–59, as cited in Ruether, "Feminist Hermeneutics," 98.

55. The selected works of Spohn examined include: *What Are They Saying about Scripture and Ethics?*; *Go and Do Likewise: Jesus and Ethics*; "Parable and Narrative in Christian Ethics," *Theological Studies* 51, no.1 (1990): 100–14; "Teaching Scripture and Ethics," *Annual of the Society of Christian Ethics* (1990): 277–81; "Jesus and Christian Ethics," *Theological Studies* 56 (1995): 92–107; "Jesus and Moral Theology," in *Moral Theology: New Directions in Fundamental Issues*, ed. James Keating (Mahwah, NJ: Paulist, 2004), 24–42; and "Scripture."

I have also consulted the following reviews: Michael G. Cartwright, *Journal of the American Academy of Religion* 70, no. 3 (Spring 2002): 678–81; John R. Donahue, "Hearers and Doers of the Word. The Challenge of William C. Spohn to Scripture and Ethics," *Explore* 10, no. 2 (Spring 2007): 10–13; Andrew J. Goddard, *Modern Believing* 41, no. 2 (April 2000): 51–52; Scott M. Lewis, *Review of Biblical Literature* 4 (2002): 351–53; Frank J. Matera, *Theological Studies* 60 (September 1999): 542–43.

56. Spohn, *Go and Do Likewise*, 27.

57. Spohn, *Go and Do Likewise*, 27–28. The relationship between virtue ethics and Scripture will be discussed in chapter 4.

58. Spohn, *Go and Do Likewise*, 164. See also "Scripture," 101.

59. Spohn, "Jesus and Christian Ethics," 102.

60. See William C. Spohn, "Jesus and Ethics," *Proceedings of the Catholic Theological Society of America* 49 (1994): 40–57.

61. Spohn, "Jesus and Christian Ethics," 101–2; Matera, review of *Go and Do Likewise*, 542.

62. For a discussion of the roles of narratives in guiding moral reflection, see Donahue, "Hearers and Doers of the Word," 11.

63. Spohn, "Parable and Narrative," 113.

64. Spohn identified the acknowledgement of presuppositions and specific interests that shape one's reading of Scripture as the first challenge. Another challenge is the move from hermeneutics to ethics.

65. The first model focuses on the experience of a Divine call in answering the fundamental question of "what ought I to do?" The second model suggests that Scripture functions as a reminder of morality that is integrally human. The third model perceives Scripture as a call to liberation and, thus, uses Scripture to support a commitment to the oppressed. The fourth model focuses on the moral agent and is convinced that Scripture is used for the transformation of the agent's identity and character. In other words, it shifts the focus from "doing" to "being." The fifth model perceives Scripture as a means through which we can discern God's love for us in Christ.

66. Spohn, *What Are They Saying about*, 95.

67. Spohn relies on the works of William Lynch and David Tracy. Specifically, Spohn is influenced by Tracy's insights on "focal meaning" that is needed for the subject to reflect analogically. See David Tracy, *The Analogical Imagination: Christian Theology and the Culture of Pluralism* (New York: Crossroad, 1981).

68. Spohn, *Go and Do Likewise*, 55.

69. Ibid., 2.

70. Spohn, "Jesus and Moral Theology," 29.

71. Martha E. Stortz, "Follow the Friendships. The Work of William Spohn," *Explore* 10, no. 2 (Spring 2007): 8.

72. James T. Bretzke, "Scripture and Ethics: Core, Context, and Coherence," in *Moral Theology: New Directions in Fundamental Issues*, ed. James Keating (Mahwah, NJ: Paulist, 2004), 103.

73. Lewis, review of *Go and Do Likewise*, 353.

74. Donahue, "Hearers and Doers of the Word," 11.

75. See Elisabeth Schüssler Fiorenza, "Discipleship and Patriarchy: Early Christian Ethos and Christian Ethics in a Feminist Theological Perspective," in *Feminist Ethics and the Catholic Moral Tradition*, ed. Charles E. Curran, Margaret A. Farley, and Richard A. McCormick (Mahwah, NJ: Paulist Press, 1996), 38–59.

76. See George M. Smiga, *The Gospel of John Set Free: Preaching Without Anti-Judaism* (Mahwah, NJ: Paulist Press, 2008), 3; Daniel

J. Harrington, *The Synoptic Gospels Set Free: Preaching Without Anti-Judaism* (Mahwah, NJ: Paulist Press, 2009), 1, 223.

Chapter 3: Moving toward a Consensus

1. My survey of Burridge's approach to biblical ethics will be based on his most recent and major works, namely, *What Are the Gospels? A Comparison with Graeco-Roman Biography* (Grand Rapids, MI: Eerdmans, and Dearborn, MI: Dove Booksellers, 2004); *Imitating Jesus: An Inclusive Approach to New Testament Ethics* (Grand Rapids, MI: Eerdmans, 2007); "Being Biblical? Slavery, Sexuality, and the Inclusive Community," *Hervormde Teologiese Studies* 64, no. 1 (March 2008): 155–74; and "Imitating Jesus: Reading the Eternal Word Response," *Scottish Journal of Theology* 63, no. 3 (August 2010): 336–52.

The following reviews and responses are also consulted: Valerie Abrahamsen, *Christian Century* 125, no. 17 (August 26, 2008): 38–39; Clarence DeWitt Agan III, *Presbyterion* 34, no. 2 (Fall 2008): 118–19; David P. Gushee, *Perspectives on Science and Christian Faith* 60, no. 3 (September 2008): 185–86; Richard B. Hays, *Scottish Journal of Theology* 63, no. 3 (August 2010): 331–35; John Paul Heil, *Theological Studies* 69, no. 4 (December 2008): 918–19; David G. Horrell, http://www.inclusivechurch2.net/Imitating-Jesus-by-Richard-Burridge-edf32f3; Ian Markham, *Scottish Journal of Theology* 63, no. 3 (August 2010): 340–45; Frank J. Matera, *Imitating Jesus: An Inclusive Approach to New Testament Ethics*, by Richard A. Burridge (Grand Rapids, MI: Eerdmans, 2007), back cover; Angus Paddison, *Studies in Christian Ethics* 22, no. 3 (2009): 382–84; Donald Senior, *Bible Today* 46, no. 2 (March–April 2008): 131–32; Graydon F. Snyder, *Sewanee Theological Review* 51, no. 4 (2008): 468–70; Charles H. Talbert, *Journal of Biblical Literature* 112, no. 4 (Winter 1993): 714–15; Francis Watson, *Scottish Journal of Theology* 63, no. 3 (August 2010): 336–39.

2. Burridge, *What Are the Gospels?* 101. Burridge gives two related reasons for focusing on Graeco-Roman biographical genre: (1) this genre has been increasingly proposed for the

Gospels; (2) it lacks proper scholarly basis and, hence, weakens its arguments.

3. Burridge, *What Are the Gospels?* 296.

4. Such a view, however, could risk the danger of separating the Gospels from their communities of origin; for the Gospels will still reflect the perspective and experience of those who produced them. Thus, one needs to distinguish the community-transcending elements from the community-specific elements and, then, discern what is important to communicate to the general audience.

5. Burridge, *What Are the Gospels?* 299.

6. Ibid., 305.

7. The importance of this book can be seen from the 2008 Annual Conference of the Society of Biblical Literature held in Boston, during which a discussion panel was set up to discuss Burridge's book.

8. Richard A. Burridge, http://www.kcl.ac.uk/artshums/depts/trs/people/staff/academic/burridge/research.aspx (accessed September 9, 2012).

9. We should note that Burridge's reference to New Testament ethics does not exhaust the scope of Christian ethics.

10. Burridge, *Imitating Jesus*, 31.

11. Burridge, "Being Biblical?" 164.

12. Ibid.,169.

13. Burridge, *Imitating Jesus*, 391.

14. Burridge, "Being Biblical?" 166.

15. Burridge, *Imitating Jesus*, 48.

16. Ibid., 154.

17. Ibid.

18. Gushee, review of *Imitating Jesus*, 185.

19. Burridge, *Imitating Jesus*, 346.

20. Gushee, review of *Imitating Jesus*, 185–86.

21. Hays further raises the question of whether inclusivity is the united ethical theme for all New Testament writings: Mark and Paul, for instance, are primarily concerned, respectively, with suffering for the sake of the Gospel and the cross that symbolizes self-giving love.

22. I understand "being inclusive" as a general description that does not necessarily mean absolute inclusivity of all.

23. Gushee, review of *Imitating Jesus*, 186.

24. Character ethics "refers to a way of thinking about and interpreting the moral life in terms of a particular vision of and a passion for life that is rooted in the nurture, formation, and socialization of a particular self-conscious community." See Walter Brueggemann, "Foreword," in *Character Ethics and the Old Testament*, ed. M. Daniel Carroll R. and Jacqueline E. Lapsley (Louisville, KY: Westminster John Knox Press, 2007), vii.

25. Matera, review of *Imitating Jesus*, back cover.

26. In this survey, only selected works of Verhey are examined: *The Great Reversal: Ethics and the New Testament* (Grand Rapids, MI: Eerdmans, 1984); *Remembering Jesus: Christian Community, Scripture, and the Moral Life* (Grand Rapids, MI: Eerdmans, 2002); *Reading the Bible in the Strange World of Medicine* (Grand Rapids, MI: Eerdmans, 2003); "The Good Samaritan and Scarce Medical Resources," *Christian Scholar's Review* 23, no. 3 (March 1994): 360–73; "Scripture and Medical Ethics: Psalm 51:10a, the Jarvik VII, and Psalm 50:9," in *Religious Methods and Resources in Bioethics*, ed. Paul F. Camenisch (Dordrecht, Netherlands: Kluwer Academic Publisher, 1994), 261–88; "The Holy Bible and Sanctified Sexuality: An Evangelical Approach to Scripture and Sexual Ethics," *Interpretation* 49, no. 1 (January 1995): 31–45; "Scripture and Ethics: Practices, Performances, and Prescriptions," in *Christian Ethics: Problems and Prospects*, ed. Lisa Sowle Cahill and James Childress (Cleveland, OH: Pilgrim Press, 1996), 18–44; "Scripture and Ethics: Canon and Community," *Union Seminary Quarterly Review* 58, no. 1–2 (2004): 13–32; "Authority and the Practice of Reading Scripture," in *Engaging Biblical Authority: Perspectives on the Bible as Scripture*, ed. William P. Brown (Louisville, KY: Westminster John Knox Press, 2007), 122–31.

The reviews consulted here include: Joseph L. Allen, *Journal of Religious Ethics* 13, no. 1 (Spring 1985): 179; Don Braxton, *Trinity Seminary Review* 25, no. 1 (Winter–Spring 2004): 43–45; James H. Burtness, *Christian Century* 102, no. 19 (May 29, 1985): 562–63; Raymond F. Collins, *Horizons* 30, no. 2 (Fall 2003): 326–28; Michael J. Gorman, *Interpretation* 57, no. 4 (October 2003): 434–37; Daniel J. Harrington, *America* 186, no. 8 (Mar 11, 2002): 25–26; Luke Timothy Johnson, *Modern Theology* 19, no. 4

(October 2003): 585–87; Andrew Lustig, *Reading the Bible in the Strange World of Medicine*, by Allen Verhey (Grand Rapids, MI: Eerdmans, 2003), back cover; David Lyall, *Expository Times* 114, no. 6 (March 2003): 210; James I. H. McDonald, *Journal of Theological Studies* 54, no. 1 (April 2003): 280–82; Walter E. Pilgrim, *Currents in Theology and Mission* 32, no. 5 (October 2005): 385–86; Donald Senior, *Theological Studies* 46 (December 1985): 736–38; *Bible Today* 40, no. 3 (May–June 2002): 198; William C. Spohn, *Theology Today* 59, no. 4 (January 2003): 652–54; Robert W. Wall, *Theology Today* 42, no. 1 (April 1985): 125–28.

27. Verhey explains that his interest in medical ethics and bioethics is closely related to his wife's career as a nurse, the technological development in medicine in the 1960s, the influence of his teachers like James M. Gustafson, as well as the inadequacy of academic writing in this area.

28. Allen Verhey, "The Use of Scripture in Moral Discourse: A Case Study of Walter Rauschenbusch" (PhD diss., Yale University, 1975).

29. Lustig, *Reading the Bible*, back cover.

30. See his *Nature and Altering It* (Grand Rapids, MI: Eerdmans, 2010); *The Christian Art of Dying: Learning from Jesus* (Grand Rapids, MI: Eerdmans, 2011).

31. In a personal conversation with Allen Verhey, during the Annual Society of Christian Ethics Conference held in San Jose, California, on January 9, 2010, Verhey claims that such recognition is a compliment; for he regards himself as an ethicist in the first place.

32. See Cahill, "Canon, Authority, Norms?" 417. In the same conversation on January 9, 2010, Verhey reveals the fact that during his time in Yale University, he first studied New Testament for two years and, then, shifted to the area of Christian ethics. This partially explains his command in biblical materials and skill in exegesis.

33. Verhey, *The Great Reversal*, 71.

34. Ibid., 86.

35. Ibid., 179.

36. Ibid., 81.

37. Wall, review of *The Great Reversal*, 128.

38. Ibid., 126.

39. Verhey, "Authority," 123, 126.

40. Verhey, "What Makes Christian Bioethics Christian? Bible, Story, and Communal Discernment," *Christian Bioethics* 11, no. 3 (December 2005): 301.

41. Verhey, "Scripture and Ethics," 28. Verhey acknowledges that his emphasis on remembering is indebted to Hauerwas's work as well.

42. Verhey, "Authority," 126.

43. Verhey, "Scripture and Ethics," 23.

44. Verhey, "Scripture and Medical Ethics," 275.

45. Verhey, "Assisted Suicide and Euthanasia: A Biblical and Reformed Perspective," in *Must We Suffer Our Way to Death? Cultural and Theological Perspectives on Death by Choice*, ed. Ronald P. Hamel and Edwin R. DuBose (Dallas, TX: Southern Methodist University Press, 1996), 230.

46. See Verhey, "Hospitality: Remembering Jesus," *Reformed Review* 57, no. 2 (Winter 2003–4), http://www.westernsem.edu/files/westernsem/Verhey.pdf; Allen Verhey, "Health and Healing in Memory of Jesus," *Ex auditu* 21 (2005): 24–48.

47. Verhey, *Remembering Jesus*, 22.

48. Ibid., 50.

49. In his essay on hospitality, Verhey likewise first posts the challenge of being hospitable to strangers. He then turns to remember Jesus who shows hospitality and becomes a stranger himself. Next, he looks at the early Church community that remembers Jesus and practices hospitality to others (e.g., Acts 2:45–46; 4:32–34). He concludes that "in memory of Jesus and in hope for God's grace, we must continue to test our traditions and performances of hospitality including our accounts of acceptable unity and diversity." Verhey, "Hospitality: Remembering Jesus," http://www.westernsem.edu/files/8712/8172/7526/win0304vol57no2.pdf.

50. There are over 1100 biblical citations listed in *Remembering Jesus*. Seven-tenths of them are from the New Testament.

51. We see a similar way of using scriptural texts in his essay on health and healing. He first employs texts from the Old Testament (e.g., 2 Chr 16:12; Sir 38:1–2) to highlight the strange world of sickness. Then, he turns to the story of Jesus who is remembered as one who heals, forgives sins, preaches the Good

News, and suffers unto death. See Verhey, "Health and Healing in Memory of Jesus," 31–41; "What Makes Christian Bioethics Christian?" 304–9.

52. Lyall, review of *Remembering Jesus*, 210.

53. Pilgrim, review of *Remembering Jesus*, 386.

54. The following discussion is based on two specific works of Verhey: "Scripture and Ethics: Practices, Performances, and Prescriptions," and "Scripture as Script and as Scripted: The Beatitudes."

55. Nicolas Wolterstorff, *Art in Action: Toward a Christian Aesthetic* (Grand Rapids, MI: Eerdmans, 1980), 80, as cited in Verhey, "Scripture as Script and as Scripted," 31 n. 2. In fact, the notions of object and instrument were first employed in his discussion of Gustafson's communal hermeneutic in 1996. See Verhey, "Scripture and Ethics: Practices," 27. Another analogy suggested by other authors is the relationship between the notes printed in a musical score, and the music played by the musician or interpreter.

56. Verhey, "Scripture as Script and as Scripted," 20.

57. Ibid., 31 n. 2.

58. Verhey, *Remembering Jesus*, 61.

59. Verhey, "Scripture as Script and as Scripted," 19.

60. Ibid., 20.

61. Ibid., 22.

62. Ibid., 28.

63. Birch and Rasmussen, *Bible and Ethics*, 7–8.

64. Ibid., 10.

65. Spohn, "Teaching Scripture and Ethics," 277.

66. See John R. Donahue and William C. Spohn, "The New Testament and Christian Ethics" (NTCE 4301 syllabus, Jesuit School of Theology at Berkeley, Berkeley, CA, Spring 1990).

67. Harrington and Keenan, *Jesus and Virtue Ethics*, 77ff.

68. See Daniel J. Harrington and James F. Keenan, "Paul and Virtue Ethics" (TH 560 syllabus, School of Theology and Ministry at Boston College, Chestnut Hill, MA, Fall 2008, 2009).

69. Daniel J. Harrington and James F. Keenan, *Paul and Virtue Ethics: Building Bridges between New Testament Studies and Moral Theology* (Lanham, MD: Rowman & Littlefield, 2010).

70. See Richard Clifford and Thomas Massaro, "Social Ethics and the Bible" (OT/MT 353 syllabus, Weston Jesuit School of Theology, Cambridge, MA, Fall 2003, 2006).

71. I am not denying the possibility of employing other hermeneutical tools in doing biblical ethics, such as a natural law framework proposed by German moral theologian Eberhard Schockenhoff. See his *Natural Law and Human Dignity*, trans. Brian McNeil (Washington, DC: The Catholic University of America Press, 2003), x.

72. William C. Mattison III, *Introducing Moral Theology: True Happiness and the Virtues* (Grand Rapids, MI: Brazos Press, 2008), 57.

73. Harrington and Keenan, *Jesus and Virtue Ethics*, xiv.

Chapter 4: A Hermeneutical Proposal

1. For this background, see Jean Porter, "Virtue Ethics," in *The Cambridge Companion to Christian Ethics*, ed. Robin Gill (Cambridge: Cambridge University Press, 2000), 96–111; "Virtue," in *The Oxford Handbook of Theological Ethics*, ed. Gilbert Meilaender and William Werpehowski (London: Oxford University Press, 2005), 205–19; William C. Spohn, "The Return of Virtue Ethics," *Theological Studies* 53, no. 1 (1992): 60–75; Joseph Woodhill, *The Fellowship of Life* (Washington, DC: Georgetown University Press, 1998), 31–45.

2. See Aristotle, *Nicomachean Ethics*, trans. J. A. K. Thomson (London: Penguin Books, 1976), 39–49.

3. Thomas Aquinas, *The Summa Theologiae of St. Thomas Aquinas*, trans. Fathers of the English Dominican Province (New York: Benziger Brothers, 1948).

4. Some perceive the resurgence as a widespread dissatisfaction with, and a protest against, those rule-, duty-, and consequence-oriented ethics. Others understand virtue theory as offering a more comprehensive picture of moral experience and standing closer to ordinary life issues than other moral philosophies; for it offers a complete vision into the complexity of moral living in the real

world. See Gilbert C. Meilaender, *The Theory and Practice of Virtue* (Notre Dame, IN: University of Notre Dame Press, 1984), 4–5.

Regarding attempts by philosophers, see Alasdair MacIntyre, "The Return to Virtue Ethics," in *The Twenty-Fifth Anniversary of Vatican II: A Look Back and a Look Ahead*, ed. Russell Smith (Braintree, MA: Pope John Center, 1990), 239–49; *After Virtue*, 3rd ed. (Notre Dame, IN: University of Notre Dame Press, 2007); Gregory Pence, "Recent Work on Virtues," *American Philosophical Quarterly* 21, no. 4 (October 1984): 281–97.

For attempts from the theological sector, see Stanley Hauerwas, *Character and the Christian Life: A Study in Theological Ethics* (San Antonio, TX: Trinity Press, 1975); *A Community of Character: Toward a Constructive Christian Social Ethic* (Notre Dame, IN: University of Notre Dame Press, 1981); James F. Keenan, *Virtues for Ordinary Christians* (Kansas City, MO: Sheed and Ward, 1996); "Proposing Cardinal Virtues," *Theological Studies* 56, no. 4 (1995): 709–29; "Virtue Ethics," in *Christian Ethics: An Introduction*, ed. Bernard Hoose (London: Chapman, 1997), 84–94; "Virtues, Principles and a Consistent Ethics of Life," in *The Consistent Ethic of Life: Assessing Its Reception and Relevance*, ed. Thomas Nairn (Maryknoll, NY: Orbis Books, 2008), 48–60; Meilaender, *The Theory and Practice of Virtue*; Pellegrino and Thomasma, *The Christian Virtues in Medical Practice*; Jean Porter, *The Recovery of Virtue* (Louisville, KY: John Knox Press, 1990).

5. Keenan, "Virtues, Principles," 50.

6. See also Robert B. Louden, "On Some Vices of Virtue Ethics," in *The Virtues: Contemporary Essays on Moral Character,"* ed. Robert B. Kruschwitz and Robert C. Roberts (Belmont, CA: Wadsworth Publishing Co., 1987), 66–73; Gregory Jones and Richard Vance, "Why Virtues Are Not Another Approach to Medical Ethics: Reconceiving the Place of Ethics in Contemporary Medicine," in *Religious Methods and Resources in Bioethics*, ed. Paul F. Camenisch (Dordrecht, Netherlands: Kluwer Academic Publishers, 1994), 203–16.

7. See Justin Oakley, "Variety of Virtue Ethics," *Ratio* 9, no. 2 (September 1996): 128–52; James F. Keenan, "Virtue and Identity," in *Creating Identity, Concilium* (2000/2), ed. Hermann

Häring, Maureen Junker-Kenny, and Dietmar Mieth (London: SCM Press, 2000), 69–77; Joseph J. Kotva, *The Christian Case for Virtue Ethics* (Washington, DC: Georgetown University Press, 1996).

8. The former treats rightness as what the agent promotes, while the latter regards rightness as what the agent honors and exemplifies. See Oakley, "Variety of Virtue Ethics," 144–51. The following brief discussion partially relies on Oakley's work, as well as Keenan's "Virtue and Identity," and Kotva's *The Christian Case.*

9. Porter, "Virtue Ethics," 107.

10. Kotva, *The Christian Case,* 17.

11. Ibid., 18.

12. James D. Wallace, "Ethics and the Craft Analogy," in *Midwest Studies in Philosophy XIII Ethical Theory: Character and Virtue,* ed. Peter A. French, Theodore E. Uehling, Jr., and Howard K. Wettstein (Notre Dame, IN: University of Notre Dame Press, 1988), 223.

13. MacIntyre, *After Virtue,* 190.

14. Kotva, *The Christian Case,* 24.

15. Ibid., 39.

16. David L. Norton, "Moral Minimalist and the Development of Moral Character," in *Midwest Studies,* ed. Finch et al., 180–81. I am in debt to Norton's own discussion here.

17. Brueggemann, "Foreword," in *Character Ethics and the Old Testament,* ed. M. Daniel Carroll R. and Jacqueline E. Lapsley (Louisville, KY: Westminster John Knox Press, 2007), vii.

18. Hauerwas, *Character and the Christian Life,* 117.

19. Norton, "Moral Minimalist," 181.

20. Ibid., 181–82.

21. William C. Spohn, *Go and Do Likewise: Jesus and Ethics* (New York: Continuum, 1999), 163.

22. MacIntyre, *After Virtue,* 187.

23. Keenan, *Virtues for Ordinary Christians,* 5.

24. Spohn, "The Return of Virtue Ethics," 67.

25. Two relevant works are specifically consulted here: Robert Adams, "Saints," in *The Virtues,* ed. Robert B. Kruschwitz and Robert C. Roberts (Belmont, CA: Wadsworth Publishing Co., 1987), 153–60; Susan Wolf, "Moral Saints," in *The Virtues,* ed.

Robert B. Kruschwitz and Robert C. Roberts (Belmont, CA: Wadsworth Publishing Co., 1987), 137–52.

26. A very new book that advocates for integration between scientific understanding of moral cognition/behavior and philosophical (and theological) virtue ethics turns to modern cognitive science in order to understand the role of exemplarity in how we learn. See James A. Van Slyke et al, eds., *Theology and the Science of Moral Action. Virtue Ethics, Exemplarity, and Cognitive Neuroscience* (Florence, KY: Routledge, 2012).

27. Meilaender, *The Theory and Practice of Virtue*, 57.

28. Woodhill, *The Fellowship of Life*, 31.

29. Spohn, *Go and Do Likewise*, 32–33.

30. Andrew Flescher, *Heroes, Saints and Ordinary Morality* (Washington, DC: Georgetown University Press, 2003), 172.

31. Ibid.

32. Ibid., 211.

33. Ibid., 219–20.

34. John Stratton Hawley, ed., "Introduction," in *Saints and Virtues* (Berkeley, CA: University of California Press, 1987), xvi, as quoted in Flescher, *Heroes, Saints and Ordinary Morality*, 177.

35. Flescher, *Heroes, Saints and Ordinary Morality*, 179.

36. Adams, "Saints," 158. See also Wolf, "Moral Saints," 137–52.

37. Kotva, *The Christian Case*, 28, 36–37. See also William C. Spohn, *What Are They Saying about Scripture and Ethics?* fully revised and expanded ed. (Mahwah, NJ: Paulist Press, 1995), 82.

38. Mark Johnson, *Moral Imagination: Implications of Cognitive Science for Ethics* (Chicago: University of Chicago, 1993), as cited in Spohn, *Go and Do Likewise*, 174.

39. Spohn, *What Are They Saying About*, 81–82.

40. MacIntyre, *After Virtue*, 273.

41. Ibid., 151.

42. Ibid., 156.

43. Keenan, "Virtues, Principles," 50.

44. Allen Verhey, *Remembering Jesus: Christian Community, Scripture, and the Moral Life* (Grand Rapids, MI: Eerdmans, 2002), 6.

45. A significant example is the debate between Lisa Sowle Cahill and Jean Porter. Cahill believes that it is not enough to rec-

ognize the emergence of norms from local cultures. Rather, it is a necessity to establish consensual universal norms among all cultures. See Lisa Sowle Cahill, "Community and Universals: A Misplaced Debate in Christian Ethics," *Annual of the Society of Christian Ethics* 18 (1998): 3–12.

46. Martha C. Nussbaum, "Non-Relative Virtues: An Aristotelian Approach," in *Midwest Studies*, ed. Finch et al., 44–45.

47. See Kotva, *The Christian Case*, 69–93.

48. See Ronald A. Mercier, "The Holy Spirit and Ethics: A Personal Gift Making Persons," in *Moral Theology: New Directions and Fundamental Issues*, ed. James Keating (Mahwah, NJ: Paulist Press, 2004), 44. Mercier's work offers a good discussion on the role of the Holy Spirit in our moral life, which I consulted here. See also Kotva, *The Christian Case*, chap. 4.

49. The following discussion is based on Kotva's *The Christian Case for Virtue Ethics*. Several reviews are also consulted: William Edgar, *Westminster Theological Journal* 60, no. 2 (Fall 1998): 42–44; C. Norman Kraus, *Mennonite Quarterly Review* 72, no. 1 (January 1998): 108; Kent Reames, *Journal of Religion* 80, no. 2 (April 2000): 353–54.

50. Kotva, *The Christian Case*, 69, 103. For Kotva, correlation does not mean merging theological elements into theoretical virtue theory but that the philosophical and theological insights correct each other, bearing in mind that there is common ground between the two. He rightly reminds us that we should not simply presume a fit between Christian convictions and virtue theory.

51. Edgar, review of *The Christian Case*, 343.

52. Kotva, *The Christian Case*, 103.

53. Ibid.

54. Ibid., 104.

55. Ibid., 105.

56. Wayne Meeks, *Moral World of First Christians* (Louisville, KY: Westminster John Knox Press, 1988), 140, as quoted in Kotva, *The Christian Case*, 116–17.

57. Edgar, review of *The Christian Case*, 343.

58. Kotva, *The Christian Case*, 117.

59. Ibid., 103.

60. The question of "who I am" is found in "those actions and attitudes that make the imperative sections necessary." See Kotva, *The Christian Case,* 128.

61. Kotva notes that many virtue ethicists emphasize the moral significance of friendship because the discussion of the shared human good requires the exploration of various relationships that are grouped under the label of "friendship."

62. Kotva, *The Christian Case,* 3.

63. For Kotva, the law exists to help shape Christian character in accordance to the virtues. Kantians, on the contrary, perceive virtue's role as enabling us to obey the moral law.

64. William C. Spohn, review of *The Christian Case for Virtue Ethics,* by Joseph Kotva, *Theological Studies* 58, no. 2 (June 1997): 398.

65. Spohn, *What Are They Saying About,* 123.

66. Spohn, *Go and Do Likewise,* 30.

67. Ibid., 31.

68. Ibid., 32.

69. Ibid.

70. Spohn, "Scripture," in *The Oxford Handbook of Theological Ethics,* ed. Gilbert Meilaender and William Werpehowski (London: Oxford University Press, 2005), 94–95.

71. Some of these issues, such as the need of grace, are also brought up by Kotva.

72. Spohn, *Go and Do Likewise,* 22.

73. Spohn, *What Are They Saying About,* 123.

74. I, hereby, elaborate and supplement what has been said about analogical imagination in chapter 2.

75. Spohn, *Go and Do Likewise,* 50.

76. Spohn, "Scripture," 99–100.

77. Spohn, "Jesus and Moral Theology," in *Moral Theology: New Directions in Fundamental Issues,* ed. James Keating (Mahwah, NJ: Paulist, 2004), 36.

78. Spohn, *Go and Do Likewise,* 60.

79. Ibid., 23.

80. Spohn, "Jesus and Moral Theology," 29–37; "Scripture," 100–101.

81. Spohn, "Jesus and Moral Theology," 29.

82. Spohn, "Scripture," 99.

83. Luke Timothy Johnson, *Decision Making in the Church: A Biblical Model* (Philadelphia, PA: Fortress Press, 1983), as cited in Spohn, "Scripture," 104.

84. The following works are particularly consulted here: John Barton, *Understanding Old Testament Ethics* (Louisville, KY: Westminster John Knox, 2003); Lisa Sowle Cahill, "Christian Character, Biblical Community, and Human Values," in *Character and Scripture: Moral Formation, Community, and Biblical Interpretation* (Grand Rapids, MI: Eerdmans, 2002), 3–17; Benjamin W. Farley, *In Praise of Virtue: An Exploration of the Biblical Virtues in a Christian Context* (Grand Rapids, MI: Eerdmans, 1995); Larry L. Rasmussen, "Sighting of Primal Visions: Community and Ecology," in *Character and Scripture: Moral Formation, Community, and Biblical Interpretation*, ed. William Brown (Grand Rapids, MI: Eerdmans, 2002), 389–409.

85. Athanasius, *The Life of Anthony* and *The Letter to Marcellinus*, trans. Robert C. Gregg, *The Classics of Western Spirituality: A Library of the Great Spiritual Masters* (New York: Paulist, 1980), 112, as quoted in Joseph Woodhill, *The Fellowship of Life* (Washington, DC: Georgetown University Press, 1998), 17. See also Keenan, "Virtue Ethics: Making a Case as It Comes of Age," *Thought* 67 (1992): 121.

86. See John W. Crossin, *What Are They Saying about Virtue?* (NY: Paulist Press, 1985), 9–10.

87. Farley, *In Praise of Virtue*, 1.

88. Bruce C. Birch and Larry L. Rasmussen, *Bible and Ethics in Christian Life*, rev. ed. (Minneapolis, MN: Augsburg, 1989), 64.

89. Crossin, *What Are They Saying about Virtue?* 10.

90. Birch and Rasmussen, *Bible and Ethics in Christian Life*, 181.

91. Barton, *Understanding Old Testament Ethics*, 72.

92. See Jens Herzer, "Paul, Job, and the New Quest for Justice," in *Character Ethics and the New Testament: Moral Dimensions of Scripture*, ed. Robert L. Brawley (Louisville, KY: Westminster John Knox, 2007), 77–79.

93. See Yiu Sing Luke (Lúcás) Chan, "A Model of Hospitality for Our Times," *Budhi: A Journal of Ideas and Culture* 10, no. 1 (2006): 1–30.

94. Cahill, "Christian Character," 10.

95. William P. Brown, ed. *Character and Scripture: Moral Formation, Community, and Biblical Interpretation* (Grand Rapids, MI: Eerdmans, 2002), xi.

96. Patrick D. Miller, "The Good Neighborhood," in *Character and Scripture: Moral Formation, Community, and Biblical Interpretation*, ed. William P. Brown (Grand Rapids, MI: Eerdmans, 2002), 58.

97. Raymond Foster, *The Restoration of Israel* (London: DLT, 1970), x.

98. Hauerwas, *A Community of Character*, 67.

Conclusion: From Bridge-Building to Integration and Dialogue

1. Carolyn Sharp and Willis Jenkins, "Scripture and Social Ethics" (REL564 syllabus, Yale Divinity School, New Haven, CT, Fall 2010).

2. Ibid.

3. Steve Pope and David Vanderhooft, "God and Morality: The Ethical Legacy of the Hebrew Bible" (TH465 syllabus, Boston College, Chestnut Hill, MA, Spring 2011).

4. Joel Green, ed., *Dictionary of Scripture and Ethics* (Grand Rapids, MI: Baker Publishing Group, 2011).

5. William C. Spohn, "The Need for Roots and Wings: Spirituality and Christian Ethics," *Theology Digest* 47 (Winter 2000): 327–40.

6. Spohn, *Go and Do Likewise*, 36.

7. Ibid., 42.

8. Richard B. Hays, review of *Go and Do Likewise: Jesus and Ethics*, by William Spohn, *Theology Today* 58, no. 4 (January 2002): 634.

9. Spohn, *Go and Do Likewise*, 3.

10. See Louis-Marie Chauvet, *Symbol and Sacrament: A Sacramental Reinterpretation of Christian Existence*, trans. Patrick Madigan and Madeleine Beaumont (Collegeville, MN: Liturgical Press, 1995), 159–316.

11. Chauvet, *Symbol and Sacrament*, 190.

12. Ibid., 263–64.

13. Ibid., 179.

14. Still, dissimilarities in terms of specific contents and fundamental conceptions need to be recognized. There exists a complex relationship between these findings, and we have to take precautions and, at times, rethink our own presuppositions in doing crosscultural ethics. See my book, *The Ten Commandments and the Beatitudes: Biblical Studies and Ethics for Real Life* (Lanham, MD: Rowman and Littlefield, 2012).

15. Confucius, *The Analects*, trans. D. C. Lau (Middlesex: Penguin Classics, 1979), 11:9, 10.

16. Mencius, *Mencius*, trans. D. C. Lau (London: Penguin Classics, 1970), 2A:6.

17. Xunzi, "A Discussion of Heaven," in *Xunzi: Basic Writings*, trans. Burton Watson (Irvington, NY: Columbia University Press, 2003), 91–110.

18. Confucius, *The Analects*, 7:9.

19. Rodney Leon Taylor, *The Religious Dimensions of Confucianism* (New York: State University of New York Press, 1990), 130.

SELECT BIBLIOGRAPHY

Achtemeier, Elizabeth. "The Impossible Possibility: Evaluating the Feminist Approach to Bible and Theology." *Interpretation* 42, no. 1 (January 1988): 45–57.

Adams, Robert. "Saints." In *The Virtues,* edited by Robert Kruschwitz and Robert Roberts, 153–60. Belmont, CA: Wadsworth Publishing Co., 1987.

Aquinas, Thomas. *The Summa Theologiae of St. Thomas Aquinas.* Translated by Fathers of the English Dominican Province. New York: Benziger Brothers, 1948.

Aristotle. *Nicomachean Ethics.* Translated by J. A. K. Thomson. London: Penguin Books, 1976.

Barton, John. *Understanding Old Testament Ethics.* Louisville, KY: Westminster John Knox, 2003.

Berquist, Jon L. "Postcolonialism and Imperial Motives for Canonization." In *The Postcolonial Biblical Reader,* edited by Rasiah S. Sugirtharajah, 78–95. Malden, MA: Blackwell, 2006.

Birch, Bruce C., and Larry L. Rasmussen. *Bible and Ethics in Christian Life.* Rev. ed. Minneapolis, MN: Augsburg, 1989.

Bretzke, James T., comp. *Bibliography on Scripture and Christian Ethics.* Lewiston, ME: E. Mellen Press, 1997.

———. *A Morally Complex World: Engaging Contemporary Moral Theology.* Collegeville, MN: Liturgical Press, 2004.

———. "Scripture and Ethics: Core, Context, and Coherence." In *Moral Theology: New Directions in Fundamental Issues,* edited by James Keating, 88–107. Mahwah, NJ: Paulist, 2004.

Brown, William P., ed. *Character and Scripture: Moral Formation, Community, and Biblical Interpretation.* Grand Rapids, MI: Eerdmans, 2002.

Burridge, Richard A. *What Are the Gospels? A Comparison with Graeco-Roman Biography*. Grand Rapids, MI: Eerdmans, and Dearborn, MI: Dove Booksellers, 2004.

———. *Imitating Jesus: An Inclusive Approach to New Testament Ethics*. Grand Rapids, MI: Eerdmans, 2007.

———. "Being Biblical? Slavery, Sexuality, and the Inclusive Community." *Hervormde Teologiese Studies* 64, no. 1 (March 2008): 155–74.

———. "Imitating Jesus: Reading the Eternal Word Response." *Scottish Journal of Theology* 63, no. 3 (August 2010): 336–52.

Cahill, Lisa Sowle. "The Bible and Ethics: Hermeneutical Dilemmas." In *Between the Sexes: Foundations for a Christian Ethics of Sexuality*, 15–44. Philadelphia, PA: Fortress Press, 1985.

———. "The New Testament and Ethics: Communities of Social Change." *Interpretation* 44, no. 4 (October 1990): 383–95.

———. "Community and Universals: A Misplaced Debate in Christian Ethics." *Annual of the Society of Christian Ethics* 18 (1998): 3–12.

———. "Christian Character, Biblical Community, and Human Values." In *Character and Scripture: Moral Formation, Community, and Biblical Interpretation*, edited by William P. Brown, 3–17. Grand Rapids, MI: Eerdmans, 2002.

Chan, Yiu-sing Luke. "A Model of Hospitality for Our Times." *Budhi: A Journal of Ideas and Culture* 10, no. 1 (2006): 1–30.

———. *The Ten Commandments and the Beatitudes: Biblical Studies and Ethics for Real Life*. Lanham, MD: Rowman and Littlefield, 2012.

Chauvet, Louis-Marie. *Symbol and Sacrament: A Sacramental Reinterpretation of Christian Existence*. Translated by Patrick Madigan and Madeleine Beaumont. Collegeville, MN: Liturgical Press, 1995.

Childress, James F. "Scripture and Christian Ethics: Some Reflections on the Role of Scripture in Moral Deliberation and Justification." *Interpretation* 34, no. 4 (October 1980): 371–80.

Confucius. *The Analects*. Translated by D. C. Lau. Middlesex: Penguin Classics, 1979.

Congregation for the Doctrine of the Faith. "Ten Observations on the Theology of Gustavo Gutiérrez." In *Liberation Theology: A Documentary History*, edited by Alfred T. Hennelly, 348–50. Maryknoll, NY: Orbis Books, 1990.

Crossin, John W. *What Are They Saying about Virtue?* New York: Paulist Press, 1985.

Curran, Charles E. "The Role and Function of the Scriptures in Moral Theology." In *Readings in Moral Theology No. 4. The Use of Scripture in Moral Theology*, edited by Charles E. Curran and Richard A. McCormick, 178–212. New York: Paulist Press, 1984.

———. "Bernard Häring: A Moral Theologian Whose Soul Matched His Scholarship." *National Catholic Reporter* 34 (July 17, 1998): 11.

———. *The Catholic Moral Tradition Today: A Synthesis*. Washington, DC: Georgetown University Press, 1999.

Curran, Charles E., and Richard A. McCormick, eds. *Readings in Moral Theology No. 4. The Use of Scripture in Moral Theology*. New York: Paulist Press, 1984.

Daly, Robert J., et al. *Christian Biblical Ethics: From Biblical Revelation to Contemporary Christian Praxis*. New York: Paulist Press, 1984.

Donahue, John R. "Hearers and Doers of the Word. The Challenge of William C. Spohn to Scripture and Ethics." *Explore* 10, no. 2 (Spring 2007): 10–13.

Duncan, William B. *The Political Philosophy of Peruvian Theologian Gustavo Gutiérrez*. Toronto Studies in Theology. Vol. 85. New York: Edwin Mellen Press, 2001.

Farley, Benjamin W. *In Praise of Virtue: An Exploration of the Biblical Virtues in a Christian Context*. Grand Rapids, MI: Eerdmans, 1995.

Fiorenza, Elisabeth Schüssler. *In Memory of Her*. New York: Crossroad, 1983.

———. "Discipleship and Patriarchy: Early Christian Ethos and Christian Ethics in a Feminist Theological Perspective." In

Feminist Ethics and the Catholic Moral Tradition, ed. Charles E. Curran, Margaret A. Farley, and Richard A. McCormick, 38–51. Mahwah, NJ: Paulist Press, 1996.

Flescher, Andrew. *Heroes, Saints and Ordinary Morality*. Washington, DC: Georgetown University Press, 2003.

Foster, Raymond. *The Restoration of Israel*. London: DLT, 1970.

Green, Joel, ed. *Dictionary of Scripture and Ethics*. Grand Rapids, MI: Baker Publishing Group, 2011.

Gustafson, James M. "The Place of Scripture in Christian Ethics: A Methodological Study." *Interpretation* 24, no. 4 (October 1970): 430–55.

Gutiérrez, Gustavo. "Freedom and Salvation." In *Liberation and Change*, edited by Ronald H. Stone, 3–96. Atlanta, GA: John Knox Press, 1977.

———. "The Irruption of the Poor in Latin America and the Christian Communities of the Common People." In *The Challenge of Basic Christian Communities*, edited by Sergio Torres and John Eagleson, and translated by John Drury, 107–23. Maryknoll, NY: Orbis Books, 1981.

———. *On Job: God-Talk and the Suffering of the Innocent*. Translated by Matthew J. O'Connell. Maryknoll, NY: Orbis Books, 1987.

———. *A Theology of Liberation*. 2nd ed. Translated and edited by Sister Caridad Inda and John Eagelson. Maryknoll, NY: Orbis Books, 1988.

———. *The Truth Shall Make You Free: Confrontations*. Translated by Matthew J. O'Connell. Maryknoll, NY: Orbis Books, 1990.

———. *God of Life*. Maryknoll, NY: Orbis Books, 1991.

Hall, Stuart. *Encoding and Decoding in the Television Discourse*. Birmingham: Centre for Cultural Studies, University of Birmingham, 1973.

Häring, Bernard. *The Law of Christ*. 3 vols. Translated by Edwin Kaiser. Westminster, MD: Newman Press, 1961, 1963, 1966.

———. "The Normative Value of the Sermon on the Mount." *Catholic Biblical Quarterly* 29 (1967): 69–79.

———. *Free and Faithful in Christ: Moral Theology for Clergy and Laity*. 3 vols. New York: Seabury Press/Crossroad, 1978, 1979, 1981.

———. "The Role of the Catholic Moral Theologian." In *Moral Theology: Challenges for the Future,* edited by Richard A. McCormick, Charles E. Curran, and Walter J. Burghardt, 32–47. Mahwah, NJ: Paulist Press, 1990.

Harrington, Daniel J. *The Synoptic Gospels Set Free: Preaching Without Anti-Judaism*. Mahwah, NJ: Paulist Press, 2009.

Harrington, Daniel J., and James Keenan. *Jesus and Virtue Ethics: Building Bridges between New Testament Studies and Moral Theology*. Chicago, IL: Sheed & Ward, 2002.

———. *Paul and Virtue Ethics: Building Bridges between New Testament Studies and Moral Theology.* Lanham, MD: Rowman and Littlefield, 2010.

Hauerwas, Stanley. *Character and the Christian Life: A Study in Theological Ethics.* San Antonio, TX: Trinity Press, 1975.

———. *A Community of Character: Toward a Constructive Christian Social Ethic.* Notre Dame, IN: University of Notre Dame Press, 1981.

Hays, Richard B. "Scripture-shaped Community: The Problem of Method in New Testament Ethics." *Interpretation* 44, no. 1 (January 1990): 42–55.

———. "New Testament Ethics. A Theological Task." *Annual of the Society of Christian Ethics* (1995): 97–120.

———. *The Moral Vision of the New Testament.* San Francisco, CA: HaperCollins, 1996.

Herzer, Jens. "Paul, Job, and the New Quest for Justice." In *Character Ethics and the New Testament: Moral Dimensions of Scripture,* edited by Robert L. Brawley, 77–86. Louisville, KY: Westminster John Knox, 2007.

Himes, Kenneth. "Scripture and Ethics: A Review Essay." *Biblical Theology Bulletin* 15, no. 2 (1985): 65–73.

Houlden, J. Leslie. *Ethics and the New Testament.* Rev. ed. Edinburgh: T&T Clark, 1992.

Johnson, Luke Timothy. *The Literary Function of Possessions in Luke-Acts.* Society of Biblical Literature Dissertation Series 39. Missoula, MT: Scholars Press, 1977.

———. "The Bible's Authority for and in the Church." In *Engaging Biblical Authority: Perspectives on the Bible as*

Scripture, edited by William P. Brown, 62–72. Louisville, KY: Westminster John Knox Press, 2007.

Jones, L. Gregory and Richard P. Vance. "Why Virtues Are Not Another Approach to Medical Ethics: Reconceiving the Place of Ethics in Contemporary Medicine." In *Religious Methods and Resources in Bioethics*, edited by Paul F. Camenisch, 203–25. Dordrecht, Netherlands: Kluwer Academic Publishers, 1994.

Keenan, James F. "Virtue Ethics: Making a Case as It Comes of Age." *Thought* 67 (1992): 115–27.

———. "Proposing Cardinal Virtues." *Theological Studies* 56, no. 4 (1995): 709–29.

———. *Virtues for Ordinary Christians*. Kansas City, MO: Sheed & Ward, 1996.

———. "Virtue Ethics." In *Christian Ethics: An Introduction*, edited by Bernard Hoose, 84–94. London: Chapman, 1997.

———. "Virtue and Identity." In *Creating Identity, Concilium* (2000/2), edited by Hermann Häring, Maureen Junker-Kenny, and Dietmar Mieth, 69–77. London: SCM Press, 2000.

———. "Virtues, Principles and a Consistent Ethics of Life." In *The Consistent Ethic of Life: Assessing its Reception and Relevance*, edited by Thomas Nairn, 48–60. Maryknoll, NY: Orbis Books, 2008.

———. *A History of Catholic Moral Theology in the Twentieth Century*. New York: Continuum, 2010.

———. "Bernard Häring's Influence on American Catholic Moral Theology." *Journal of Moral Theology* 1, no. 1 (2012): 23–42.

Kotva, Joseph J. *The Christian Case for Virtue Ethics*. Washington, DC: Georgetown University Press, 1996.

Kwok, Pui-lan. "Making the Connections: Postcolonial Studies and Feminist Biblical Interpretation." In *The Postcolonial Biblical Reader*, edited by Rasiah S. Sugirtharajah, 45–63. Malden, MA: Blackwell, 2006.

Lohse, Eduard. *Theological Ethics of the New Testament*. Translated by M. Eugene Boring. Minneapolis, MN: Fortress Press, 1991.

Louden, Robert B. "On Some Vices of Virtue Ethics." In *The Virtues: Contemporary Essays on Moral Character*, edited by Robert B. Kruschwitz and Robert C. Roberts, 66–73. Belmont, CA: Wadsworth Publishing Co., 1987.

MacIntyre, Alasdair. "The Return to Virtue Ethics." In *The Twenty-Fifth Anniversary of Vatican II: A Look Back and a Look Ahead*, edited by Russell Smith, 239–49. Braintree, MA: Pope John Center, 1990.

———. *After Virtue*. 3rd ed. Notre Dame, IN: University of Notre Dame Press, 2007.

MacNamara, Vincent. *Faith and Ethics: Recent Roman Catholicism*. Washington, DC: Georgetown University Press, 1985.

Matera, Frank J. "Matthew 27: 11–54." *Interpretation* 38, no. 1 (January 1984): 55–59.

———. "The Death of Jesus According to Luke: A Question of Sources." *Catholic Biblical Quarterly* 47 (July 1985): 469–85.

———. "Responsibility for the Death of Jesus according to the Acts of the Apostles." *Journal for the Study of the New Testament* 39 (June 1990): 77–93.

———. "Ethics for the Kingdom of God: The Gospel according to Mark." *Louvain Studies* 20, no. 2–3 (Summer–Fall 1995): 187–200.

———. *New Testament Ethics: The Legacies of Jesus and Paul*. Louisville, KY: Westminster John Knox, 1996.

———. "Galatians and the Development of Paul's Teaching on Justification." *Word & World* 20, no. 3 (Summer 2000): 239–48.

———. "New Testament Theology: History, Method, and Identity." *Catholic Biblical Quarterly* 67, no. 1 (January 2005): 1–21.

———. "Christ in the Theologies of Paul and John." *Theological Studies* 67, no. 2 (June 2006): 237–56.

Mattison III, William C. *Introducing Moral Theology: True Happiness and the Virtues*. Grand Rapids, MI: Brazos Press, 2008.

Meilaender, Gilbert C. *The Theory and Practice of Virtue*. Notre Dame, IN: University of Notre Dame Press, 1984.

Meier, John P. "The Bible as Source of Theology." *CTSA Proceedings* 43 (1988): 1–14.

Mencius. *Mencius*. Translated by D. C. Lau. London: Penguin Classics, 1970.

Mercier, Ronald A. "The Holy Spirit and Ethics: A Personal Gift Making Persons." In *Moral Theology: New Directions and Fundamental Issues*, edited by James Keating, 43–68. Mahwah, NJ: Paulist Press, 2004.

Miller, Patrick D. "The Good Neighborhood." In *Character and Scripture: Moral Formation, Community, and Biblical Interpretation*, edited by William P. Brown, 55–72. Grand Rapids, MI: Eerdmans, 2002.

Norton, David L. "Moral Minimalist and the Development of Moral Character." In *Midwest Studies in Philosophy XIII Ethical Theory: Character and Virtue*, edited by Peter A. French, Theodore E. Uehling, Jr., and Howard K. Wettstein, 180–95. Notre Dame, IN: University of Notre Dame Press, 1988.

Nussbaum, Martha C. "Non-Relative Virtues: An Aristotelian Approach." In *Midwest Studies in Philosophy XIII Ethical Theory: Character and Virtue*, edited by Peter A. French, Theodore E. Uehling, Jr., and Howard K. Wettstein, 32–53. Notre Dame, IN: University of Notre Dame Press, 1988.

Oakley, Justin. "Variety of Virtue Ethics." *Ratio* 9, no. 2 (September 1996): 128–52.

Odozor, Paulinus Ikechukwu. *Moral Theology in an Age of Renewal*. Notre Dame, IN: University of Notre Dame Press, 2003.

Ogletree, Thomas W. *The Use of the Bible in Christian Ethics: A Constructive Essay*. Philadelphia, PA: Fortress Press, 1983.

Pellegrino, Edmund D., and David C. Thomasma. *The Christian Virtues in Medical Practice*. Washington, DC: Georgetown University Press, 1996.

Pence, Gregory E. "Recent Work on Virtues." *American Philosophical Quarterly* 21, no. 4 (October 1984): 281–97.

Perkins, Pheme. *Love Commands in the New Testament*. New York: Paulist Press, 1982.

———. "New Testament Ethics: Questions and Contexts." *Religious Studies Review* 10 (October 1984): 321–27.

Pontifical Biblical Commission. *The Bible and Morality: Biblical Roots of Christian Conduct.* Vatican: Libreria Editrice Vaticana, 2008.

Porter, Jean. *The Recovery of Virtue*. Louisville, KY: John Knox Press, 1990.

———. "Virtue Ethics." In *The Cambridge Companion to Christian Ethics*, edited by Robin Gill, 96–111. Cambridge: Cambridge University Press, 2000.

———. "Virtue." In *The Oxford Handbook of Theological Ethics*, edited by Gilbert Meilaender and William Werpehowski, 205–19. London: Oxford University Press, 2005.

Rasmussen, Larry L. "Sighting of Primal Visions: Community and Ecology." In *Character and Scripture: Moral Formation, Community, and Biblical Interpretation*, edited by William P. Brown, 389–409. Grand Rapids, MI: Eerdmans, 2002.

Reiter, Johannes. "Die Katholische Moraltheologie Zwischen den Beiden Vatikanischen Konzils." In *Die Katholischtheologische Disziplinen in Deutschland 1870–1962. Ihre Geschichte, ihre Zeitbezug*, edited by Hubert Wolf, 231–42. Paderborn: Schöningh, 1999.

Rowe, C. Kavin. "New Testament Theology: The Revival of a Discipline." *Journal of Biblical Literature* 125 (2006): 393–410.

Ruether, Rosemary Radford. *Mary: The Feminine Face of the Church.* Philadelphia, PA: The Westminster Press, 1977.

———. "Feminism and Patriarchal Religion: Principles of Ideological Critique of the Bible." *Journal for the Study of the Old Testament* 22 (Fall 1982): 54–66.

———. *Sexism and God-Talk*. Boston, MA: Beacon Press, 1983.

———. "The Future of Feminist Theology." *Journal of the American Academy of Religion* 53, no. 4 (December 1985): 703–13.

———. "Feminist Interpretation: A Method of Correlation." In *Feminist Interpretation of the Bible*, edited by Letty M. Russell, 111–24. Philadelphia, PA: The Westminster Press, 1985.

———. *Disputed Questions: On Being a Christian*. Maryknoll, NY: Orbis Books, 1989.

———. "Feminist Hermeneutics, Scriptural Authority, and Religious Experience: The Case of the *Imago Dei* and Gender Equality." In *Radical Pluralism and Truth*, edited by Werner G. Jeanrond and Jennifer L. Rike, 95–106. New York: Crossroad, 1991.

———. "Imago Dei, Christian Tradition and Feminist Hermeneutics." In *Image of God and Gender Models in Judaeo-Christian Tradition*, edited by Kari Elizabeth Børresen, 258–81. Oslo: Solum Forlag, 1991.

———. *Gaia and God: An Ecofeminist Theology of Earth Healing*. San Francisco, CA: HarperSanFrancisco, 1992.

Sanders, Jack T. *Ethics in the New Testament*. London: SCM Press Ltd, 1976.

Schneiders, Sandra M. "Faith, Hermeneutics, and the Literal Sense of Scripture." *Theological Studies* 39, no. 4 (December 1978): 719–36.

———. "From Exegesis to Hermeneutics: The Problem of the Contemporary Meaning of Scripture." *Horizons: Journal of the College Theology Society* 8 (Spring 1981): 23–39.

———. "The Paschal Imagination: Objectivity and Subjectivity in New Testament Interpretation." *Theological Studies* 43 (March 1982): 52–68.

———. "New Testament Reflections on Peace and Nuclear Arms." In *Catholics and Nuclear War: A Commentary on the Challenge of Peace, the U.S. Catholic Bishops' Pastoral Letter on War and Peace*, edited by Philip J. Murnion, 91–105. New York: Crossroad Publishing Co, 1983.

———. "Church and Biblical Scholarship in Dialogue." *Theology Today* 42, no. 3 (October 1985): 353–58.

———. "John 20: 11–18: The Encounter of the Easter Jesus with Mary Magdalene—A Transformative Feminist Reading." In *What is John? Readers and Readings of the Fourth Gospel*, edited by Fernando F. Segovia, 155–68. Atlanta, GA: Scholars Press, 1996.

———. *The Revelatory Text: Interpreting the New Testament as Sacred Scripture*. Collegeville, MN: Liturgical Press, 1999.

———. *Written That You May Believe: Encountering Jesus in the Fourth Gospel*. New York: Crossroad Publishing, 1999.

Schockenhoff, Eberhard. *Natural Law and Human Dignity.* Translated by Brian McNeil. Washington, DC: The Catholic University of America Press, 2003.

Schubeck, Thomas L. *Liberation Ethics: Sources, Models, and Norms.* Minneapolis, MN: Fortress Press, 1993.

Siker, Jeffrey S. *Scripture and Ethics: Twentieth-Century Portraits.* New York: Oxford University Press, 1997.

Van Slyke, James A., et al., eds. *Theology and the Science of Moral Action. Virtue Ethics, Exemplarity, and Cognitive Neuroscience.* Florence, KY: Routledge, 2012.

Smiga, George M. *The Gospel of John Set Free: Preaching Without Anti-Judaism.* Mahwah, NJ: Paulist Press, 2008.

Spohn, William C. "The Use of Scripture in Moral Theology." *Theological Studies* 47, no. 1 (1986): 88–102.

———. "Parable and Narrative in Christian Ethics." *Theological Studies* 51, no. 1 (1990): 100–14.

———. "Teaching Scripture and Ethics." *Annual of the Society of Christian Ethics* (1990): 277–81.

———. "The Return of Virtue Ethics." *Theological Studies* 53, no. 1 (1992): 60–75.

———. "Jesus and Ethics." *Proceedings of the Catholic Theological Society of America* 49 (1994): 40–57.

———. *What Are They Saying about Scripture and Ethics?* Fully revised and expanded ed. Mahwah, NJ: Paulist Press, 1995.

———. "Jesus and Christian Ethics." *Theological Studies* 56 (1995): 92–107.

———. *Go and Do Likewise: Jesus and Ethics.* New York: Continuum, 1999.

———. "The Need for Roots and Wings: Spirituality and Christian Ethics." *Theology Digest* 47 (Winter 2000): 327–40.

———. "Jesus and Moral Theology." In *Moral Theology: New Directions in Fundamental Issues,* edited by James Keating, 24–42. Mahwah, NJ: Paulist, 2004.

———. "Scripture." In *The Oxford Handbook of Theological Ethics*, edited by Gilbert Meilaender and William Werpehowski, 93–111. London: Oxford University Press, 2005.

Stortz, Martha E. "Follow the Friendships. The Work of William Spohn." *Explore* 10, no. 2 (Spring 2007): 4–9.

Sugirtharajah, Rasiah S. "Introduction, and Some Thoughts on Asian Biblical Hermeneutics." *Biblical Interpretation* 2, no. 3 (1994): 251–63.

———. *Asian Biblical Hermeneutics and Postcolonialism: Contesting the Interpretations.* Sheffield: Sheffield Academic Press, 1999.

———. *The Bible and the Third World: The Precolonial, Colonial and Postcolonial Encounters.* New York: Cambridge University Press, 2001.

———. *Postcolonial Criticism and Biblical Interpretation.* New York: Oxford University Press, 2002.

———. ed. *The Postcolonial Biblical Reader.* Malden, MA: Blackwell, 2006.

———. "Introduction: Empires Old and New." In *The Postcolonial Biblical Reader*, edited by Rasiah S. Sugirtharajah, 67–68. Malden, MA: Blackwell, 2006.

———. "The First, Second and Third Letters of John." In *A Postcolonial Commentary on the New Testament Writings*, edited by Fernando Segovia and Rasiah S. Sugirtharajah, 413–23. New York: T&T Clark, 2007.

Tambasco, Anthony J. "First and Third World Ethics." In *Christian Biblical Ethics: From Biblical Revelation to Contemporary Christian Praxis*, edited by Robert J. Daly et al., 139–55. New York: Paulist Press, 1984.

Taylor, Rodney Leon. *The Religious Dimensions of Confucianism.* New York: State University of New York Press, 1990.

Tracy, David. *The Analogical Imagination: Christian Theology and the Culture of Pluralism*. New York: Crossroad, 1981.

Vatican II. *Optatam Totius*. Decree on priestly training, October 1965. http://www.vatican.va/archive/hist_councils/ii_vatican_council/documents/vat-ii_decree_19651028_optatam-totius_en.html.

Verhey, Allen. *The Great Reversal: Ethics and the New Testament.* Grand Rapids, MI: Eerdmans, 1984.

———. "The Good Samaritan and Scarce Medical Resources." *Christian Scholar's Review* 23, no. 3 (March 1994): 360–73.

———. "Scripture and Medical Ethics: Psalm 51:10a, the Jarvik VII, and Psalm 50:9." In *Religious Methods and Resources in Bioethics,* edited by Paul F. Camenisch, 261–88. Dordrecht, Netherlands: Kluwer Academic Publisher, 1994.

———. "The Holy Bible and Sanctified Sexuality: An Evangelical Approach to Scripture and Sexual Ethics." *Interpretation* 49, no. 1 (January 1995): 31–45.

———. "Assisted Suicide and Euthanasia: A Biblical and Reformed Perspective." In *Must We Suffer Our Way to Death?: Cultural and Theological Perspectives on Death by Choice,* edited by Ronald P. Hamel and Edwin R. DuBose, 226–65. Dallas, TX: Southern Methodist University Press, 1996.

———. "Scripture and Ethics: Practices, Performances, and Prescriptions." In *Christian Ethics: Problems and Prospects,* edited by Lisa Sowle Cahill and James Childress, 18–44. Cleveland, OH: Pilgrim Press, 1996.

———. *Remembering Jesus: Christian Community, Scripture, and the Moral Life.* Grand Rapids, MI: Eerdmans, 2002.

———. *Reading the Bible in the Strange World of Medicine.* Grand Rapids, MI: Eerdmans, 2003.

———. "Hospitality: Remembering Jesus." *Reformed Review (Online)* 57, no. 2 (Winter 2003–2004): http://www.westernsem.edu/files/westernsem/Verhey.pdf (accessed September 25, 2009).

———. "Scripture and Ethics: Canon and Community." *Union Seminary Quarterly Review* 58, no. 1–2 (2004): 13–32.

———. "Health and Healing in Memory of Jesus." *Ex auditu* 21 (2005): 24–48.

———. "Authority and the Practice of Reading Scripture." In *Engaging Biblical Authority: Perspectives on the Bible as Scripture,* edited by William P. Brown, 122–31, 152–54. Louisville, KY: Westminster John Knox Press, 2007.

———. "Scripture as Script and as Scripted: The Beatitudes." In *Character Ethics and the New Testament: Moral Dimensions of Scripture*, edited by Robert L. Brawley, 19–34. Louisville, KY: Westminster John Knox, 2007.

———. *Nature and Altering It*. Grand Rapids, MI: Eerdmans, 2010.

———. *The Christian Art of Dying: Learning from Jesus*. Grand Rapids, MI: Eerdmans, 2011.

Wallace, James D. "Ethics and the Craft Analogy." In *Midwest Studies in Philosophy XIII Ethical Theory: Character and Virtue*, ed. Peter A. French, Theodore E. Uehling, Jr., and Howard K. Wettstein, 222–32. Notre Dame, IN: University of Notre Dame Press, 1988.

Wolf, Susan. "Moral Saints." In *The Virtues*, edited by Robert Kruschwitz and Robert Roberts, 137–52. Belmont, CA: Wadsworth Publishing Co., 1987.

Woodhill, Joseph. *The Fellowship of Life*. Washington, DC: Georgetown University Press, 1998.

Xunzi. *Xunzi: Basic Writings*. Translated by Burton Watson. Irvington, NY: Columbia University Press, 2003.

INDEX